Am I Living a Spiritual Life?

Susan Muto and Adrian van Kaam

Am I Living a Spiritual Life?

Questions and Answers
for Those Who Pray

SOPHIA INSTITUTE PRESS®
Manchester, New Hampshire

Am I Living a Spiritual Life? is a revised version of the original edition, published in 1978 by Dimension Books, Inc., Denville, New Jersey.

Copyright © 2006 Epiphany Association,
Susan Muto and Adrian van Kaam

Printed in the United States of America

Biblical citations are taken from the Revised Standard Version of the Bible (© 1971 by Division of Christian Education of the National Council of the Churches of Christ in the United States of America).

Cover design by Theodore Schluenderfritz

Sophia Institute Press®
Box 5284, Manchester, NH 03108
1-800-888-9344
www.sophiainstitute.com

Imprimi potest: Rev. Philip J. Haggerty, C.S.Sp., Provincial
Nihil obstat: Rev. William J. Winter, S.T.D., *Censor librorum*
Imprimatur: Most Rev. Vincent M. Leonard, D.D.,
Bishop of Pittsburgh
June 1978

Library of Congress Cataloging-in-Publication Data

Muto, Susan Annette.
    Am I living a spiritual life? : questions and answers
for those who pray / by Susan Muto and Adrian
van Kaam ; foreword by Adrian van Kaam. — [Rev. version].
        p. cm.
    ISBN-13: 978-1-933184-21-0 (pbk. : alk. paper)
    1. Spiritual life — Catholic Church — Miscellanea.
    I. Van Kaam, Adrian L., 1920- II. Title.

BX2350.3.M878 2006
248.4'82 — dc22   2006008796

10 9 8 7 6 5 4 3 2

Contents

Part 1
Developing a Spiritual Life

Part 2
Integrating Prayer and Participation

Part 3
Living Christian Community

☞

Foreword

by Adrian van Kaam

All people are called to discover the unique form God wants to give to their lives. For Christians this means that they have to find their unique life form in Christ. It's not only a question of gradually discovering the form my life has to take but of allowing my daily existence to be an answer to this call.

My deepest desire is to be someone unique who lasts forever. A secret yearning for eternity wells up from the core of my being. I seek something lasting amidst the transitoriness of my countless self-expressions. What lasts is my spiritual or fundamental self. This core self isn't of my own making; it's God's gift to me, not a gift that I have but the gift that I am. God first loved me into being as a new emergent self, unique on this earth. He continues to call me lovingly to the unique-communal life form meant for me from eternity. I must answer this call to be myself by commitment and ongoing self-formation, by a life that offers to God a wholehearted yes. This yes to the gift and burden of ongoing self-formation is the foundation of my spiritual life.

For most of us the formative meaning of life reveals itself only bit by bit in the act of living. As I ponder in prayerful presence what happens to me, in me, and around me, slowly a certain direction might emerge. I see a line; a hidden consistency makes itself known. The more this direction clarifies itself, the more I become aware of what kind of self-formation is in harmony with the heart of my existence.

In the center of my being, God keeps communicating to me in love the true form he wants my life to take. He speaks mainly through the circumstances he allows in my life. This book is meant to help you remain in dialogue with this voice of the Lord. Its aim is to assist you in finding the thread that holds the events of life together in this graced disclosure of what God calls you to be. I'm not forced to say yes to this gift of disclosure. God's call in the life situation doesn't compel a response. He waits with infinite gentleness and patience for my reply.

The mystery of my deepest identity can't be found by means of a test or a clinical interview. The ultimate guide I have is the underlying consistency of my life and its harmony with scripture, Church doctrine, and the wisdom of the spiritual masters. As I discover increasingly who I am before God, my life becomes more consistent. In the light of doctrine, the scriptures, traditional wisdom, and personal inspiration, I can come to see what is the best option among the different life choices offered to me. This book illustrates this path by reflections on the many questions people ask themselves while seeking their way in the situations they face daily. We hope these questions and answers will help you to be more in touch with yourself and your hidden calling.

I might not always be able to defend my options with arguments that can't be refuted by the rational mind. It might be impossible for others to understand that a choice I made can be right for me. It's only in the long run that a chain of inspired decisions might begin to make sense. They become meaningful in the total formative orientation that my emergent self begins to manifest.

It's often only in retrospect that people discover the hidden consistency of the many seemingly disparate choices they've made over a long period.

One condition for the ongoing discovery of the form my life should take in the eyes of God is the ability to distance myself from the circumstances in which I find myself or from the problems or tasks in which I'm involved. I must grasp who I'm called to be both in and beyond my actual life situation. The responses in this book to similar questions by believers and sincere seekers can help you to gain this ability for distancing in service of deeper self-formation. If there are apparent changes in my life, it isn't because God's call has changed but because my knowledge of this call has expanded and deepened during the history of my self-formation. Since I can't know and enflesh my call at once, formation is ongoing; it's never achieved but is forever being achieved.

To find the life form that best expresses the call of the Lord, I might have to go through the way of trial and error. Before I commit myself to an answer to the question any life situation poses, I have to ask what answer is really the best one for me. The necessity of wise questioning can lead to a crisis. All commitment evokes the fear of making a mistake. Because of this fear, I might get stuck in an excessively prolonged period of trial and error. In that case I might not come to an answer at all. The impulsive attempt to end the period of doubt prematurely by a sudden willful decision only makes matters worse.

Both excessive delay and impulsive decision might imply unfaithfulness to our unique-communal life call. This book presents responses based on universal human experience so that you may neither delay your answer to the situation nor respond impulsively without sufficient prayerful reflection and the graced guidance of the Holy Spirit.

Acknowledgments

For her invaluable help in reading the manuscript and offering welcome corrections and additions to the text that drew out with further clarity its meaning, we thank our friend Mrs. John Otis Carney. Together with Mrs. Carney's contribution, we gratefully acknowledge the combined work done by Vicki Bittner and Mary Lou Perez and the *Envoy* work done by the following students, research associates, and graduates of our Institute of Formative Spirituality: Sr. Una Agnew, SSL; Sr. Elizabeth Berrigan CSJ; Sr. Andree Bindewald, O. Carm; Sr. Goretti Blank, SDR; Rev. Ray P. Bomberger, SSJ; Sr. Claire Brissette, SSCh; Sr. Joan Michael Carboy, SSJ; Sr. Rosemarie Carfagna, OSU; Sr. Marie Chin, RSM; Rev. Charles Cummings, OCSO; Sr. Bernardine Dirkx, SSM; Sr. Regina Marie Dubickas, SSC; Sr. Martin de Porres Fernandes, OP; Sr. Marianne Flory, SCJ; Sr. Janice Fulmer, CSFN; Sr. Charlotte Girard, SCJ; Sr. Ellen Guerin, RSM; Sr. Mary Cecile Gunelson, CPPS; Sr. Sheila Harron, RSM; Sr. Maria del Carmen Hernandez, CCVI; Br. Denis Hever, FMS; Sr. Mary Germaine Hustedde, PHJC; Sr. M. Sharon Iacobucci, CSSF; Sr. Jeanne Jezik, OSF; Sr. Carol Ann Jokerst, CCVI; Sr. Grace Jordan, SSL; Sr. Maureen Kelly, SSL; Rev. Paul Keyes; Sr. Marie Kruszewski, CSFN; Sr. Victoria Lane, OSM; Sr. Alice Laferriere, SASV; Sr. Therese Leckert,

OP; Sr. Brenda Mary Lynch, SSND; Sr. Kathleen Lyons, CSJ; Sr. Mary McKay, CSJ; Sr. Lucille Meissen, CPPS; Sr. Mary Mester, RSM; Sr. Agatha Muggli, OSB; Sr. Gertrude Mulholland, SSIC; Sr. Marian Murray, SHG; Sr. Lillian Needham, SSJ; Rev. Harry Neely, OSA; Sr. Mairead O'Reardon, OSF; Sr. Gemma Pepera, CSFN; Sr. Kathleen Power, SSJ; Sr. Mary Price, SC; Rev. William Sheehan, OMI; Sr. Sarah Marie Sherman, RSM; Sr. Marcella Springer, SSJ; Sr. Kathleen Storms, SSND; Sr. Celine Thames, FMI; Rev. James Thompson, OSA; Sr. Mary Fidelis Tracy, CDP; Sr. Jeanne Marie Ulica, OSF; and Sr. Anita Viens, SSCH.

Am I Living a Spiritual Life?

Part 1

Developing a Spiritual Life

Am I Living a Spiritual Life?

In living a spiritual life, there are so many
obstacles to avoid, so many conditions to
fulfill, so much trust in God to maintain.
What assurance is there that I'm approaching
God more closely and not merely deceiving myself?

How easily we can slip into self-satisfaction in our spiritual growth! I remember that morning after Mass and prayers when I had been so devout! My meditation flowed so smoothly! Surely these were signs that I must be growing in the spiritual life. But later that morning I barked at my secretary and didn't apologize when I realized I had been in the wrong. That made me stop and think. If I were growing closer to God in prayer, wouldn't I manifest the power of this growth more regularly in daily life?

There can be no complete assurance that we're approaching God more closely. However, reflection on the way we live can give us an indication of whether we're trying to develop a spiritual life or only deluding ourselves.

Our Lord reminds us in the Gospel that we can tell a good tree from a bad tree by the fruit it produces (cf. Matt. 7:17-20).

Am I Living a Spiritual Life?

Keeping this text in mind, we can appraise our life by asking, "Does it bear fruit spiritually?"

What I do in my life is an indicator of whether I live for God or for myself alone. If Christ, not I, is the center of my life, one effect will be compassion for my neighbor. Neighbor means not just the person next door but the members of my family, students and co-workers, even strangers. At home with Christ, I feel more at one with others. They see in me a witness of God's love for them.

Despite my efforts I might fail time and again, but if I live for him, I can overlook these stumblings. With his help, love becomes the source of my spiritual life, the light of my service.

Growth is difficult to measure because it can't be seen. At the start of each new season a mother stores the clothing worn in the summer or autumn just ended and brings out items for the season at hand. She exclaims with dismay that last season's clothing doesn't fit the children anymore. Yet she was scarcely aware of how much they had grown during the past several months.

What a surprise when I notice the ivy on my windowsill. On a Tuesday it might look like a struggling twig, but when I water it on Friday I'm surprised to see the beginning of several new leaves. Growth has occurred silently, imperceptibly.

The growth that can be seen by trousers that are too short or by a new leaf ready to open is apparent only after it has happened. Although we might speak loosely of seeing something grow before our eyes, we're talking about what has happened as a result of growth rather than about the process of growth itself.

In both examples, there are certain conditions that have fostered the development we behold. Balanced diet, freedom from illness, and sufficient sleep and exercise help children to grow; sunlight, water, and fresh air foster the ivy's blooming. Growth is a mysterious process we can facilitate but not control.

Growth in the spiritual life is in some ways like the growth that we experience physically and mentally. In the life of the spirit too, certain conditions foster nearness to God, such as inner silence, fidelity to prayer, recollection, and ascetical practices. All of these ordinary spiritual exercises occur within the confines of daily life.

We might be aware of alterations in our relationship with God — for example, a movement toward more reposeful prayer, a dryness and absence of delight, or a truer charity in service of others. We might experience the mysteriousness of this growth and realize that no amount of desire, willing, or manipulating can do more than prepare for the gift of further unfolding.

Growth in the spiritual life wells up from within. It can't be felt or seen. We'll never know with certainty that we're becoming spiritually mature. Uncertainty shouldn't cause us anguish; it should be an occasion for trust in the Lord alone. He who sees my heart's desire, who loves me more than I love myself, will give me the grace of growth in his own way and time.

Unlike temperature, spirituality resists measurement. For example, my room feels frigid, so I consult the thermometer. Sixty degrees. I return to my desk and try to study. Although the crackle of the radiator tells me that the heat is coming up, I still distract myself by again consulting the thermometer. Sixty-five. Seventy. Now I feel comfortable, although all I had accomplished when altering this device was to compound my uncomfortable feeling.

In fact, preoccupation with the progress I might or might not be making in the spiritual life can be a hindering rather than a facilitating factor. When I attempt to measure the degree of my spirituality, I become introspective. My "executive will," not the Divine Will, becomes central. I want to know how I'm doing. The emphasis is on me, not on God. Spirituality is seen not as a gift but as a project. I look backward to the ground I've covered and try to measure the distance already traversed.

The author of *The Cloud of Unknowing* tells us the opposite: Look ahead, he says, not behind. See what you still lack, not what you already have; this is the quickest way of gaining humility. Our whole life must be one of longing if we're to achieve union with God.

God wants us to take the simple reality of every day and believe in it. Spirituality is true if it emerges from the context of living my daily situation as God's will for me. This everydayness, common-place as it is, is the truest measure of the spiritual life.

Prayerful reflection is necessary so that we won't confuse growth with activity; intimacy with fantasy; openness to the Spirit with self-induced placidity.

In prayer we come to recognize Christ as the Source of our life. He radiates his mercy through our actions. Our life is his gift. Day by day we try to live in grateful awareness of this gift, letting each situation bring forth a new opportunity for love.

During moments of meditation, we might not "feel" our rooted-ness in the Lord. We might be unsure whether we've prayed or not, but we believe Christ dwells in our hearts, even in dryness.

To be on the way toward him is to live in faith even when I'm not feeling anything, to obey his will even when everyday routine seems disappointing. The uncertainty I feel is precisely what calls me back to him again and again. Rather than become overly con-cerned with progress in the spiritual life, I choose to let this uncer-tainty be, understanding it as God's will for me at this time — as a message inviting me to return to his presence in faith.

An old priest was once asked the same question: "How do you know when you're coming closer to God?" He chuckled. "You know it when you're doing his will. You just know it."

"You just know it." His reply came without hesitation and with the confidence of a lifetime of experience. He didn't stop and think, nor did he enter into a lengthy discussion. His simple answer reflects a personal understanding of the spiritual life, one that we, in our competitive, data-conscious world, tend to forget.

There are various ways of knowing, including the knowledge of intellectual certitude, of logical, cause-effect principles, but it fails when we try to use such techniques to evaluate our relationship with God.

The phrase "coming closer to God" means "becoming aware of God," for we are already close to him. St. Paul tells us, ". . . he is not far from each of us, for in him we live and move and have our being . . ." (Acts 17:27-28). Becoming a more spiritual person means becoming aware of our rootedness in God, of our dependence on him for every breath we take, every thought we have.

Daily concerns draw our attention away from this reality. We have to prepare classes, plan meals, look after business and family dealings. Behind and supporting all of these involvements is the spiritual reality that these people, events, and things are maintained in their existence by a loving, caring Father. Since the immediacy of daily life tends to hold our attention, we need to increase our awareness of Christ's presence, of his secret plan for us behind all our human projects.

The effort isn't easy. Only the "little ones of God" seem to be graced with an ability to be busy with daily cares while being fully attentive to God's presence. The rest of us are usually absorbed by immediate involvements. To set aside special times each day, each month, each year to recollect ourselves in meditation and reflective reading is our only alternative. Such times help us grow attentive to God's loving will. We become more aware of the closeness that's already there.

Gradually our fidelity to these exercises moves us nearer to finding God's plan for our lives. Although our daily involvements still demand attention, they're no longer isolating and fragmenting. In them we see God's love for us and an opportunity to grow in loving response to him. The people we serve, the dreams we dream, the relaxed and anxious moments we have still remain in the foreground of our experience; but we can, with God's grace, see them in a new light.

This encounter of the soul and God is comparable to the mutual loving awareness of bride and groom. As they plan their life together, the values, preferences, and interests of each of them form the backdrop against which both of them make decisions that are mutually beneficial.

God, far more than any earthly love, wills our good. He is the source and support of our whole life. He is always close to us, closer than we can imagine. We need only become attentive to this closeness, given to us gratuitously. Our yes to this gift is the measure of our becoming spiritually mature.

2

Listening to Our Life Call

If our life call comes from God, how can we discern it?
Is it a matter of listening to God speaking in the
depths of our soul and responding to this grace?
What if we refuse to follow this directive?

When I have to make a decision, especially a serious one, I consult others whose knowledge and experience exceed my own. To discover God's will also implies an openness to what others can tell me. Choosing my calling depends not only on me and God, but also on God speaking in my situation.

Others who know me and my history might be able to help me to discern whether my judgment is sound. Relying only on my own perception to appraise my life direction might not be the wisest move.

For example, a girl might apply for entrance to a religious community convinced that she's responding to her calling. After much testing, consultation, and guidance, the director of vocations decides that she's better suited for celibate life in the world, or perhaps for the married life. This judgment isn't an indictment of failure but a response to facts. The call to holiness can be concretized in a variety of forms and styles. Finding the right one is important, so it might be wise to seek help. This person might truly be called to a life of intimate union with God but not necessarily in the religious state.

If the vocation director believes this girl will not be happy in religious life, the only caring response is to tell her so. If the girl persists in believing that she should be allowed to enter, the director still has the right, and indeed the obligation, to deny her this request. She might not make her decision with absolute certainty; in fact, she might suffer agonizing doubts, but, according to her insights into this person and the demands of religious living in this community, she must decide yes or no.

Not to decide is an evasion of responsibility. Since a religious vocation involves not just one person but a community and a shared future, it would be unrealistic for a vocation director to say, "Do what you think is best. Who am I to disagree?"

In appraising the life direction of others, it's necessary to take into account their personality development; their degree of emotional stability; their ability to relate to others; the quality of their prayer life; the balance they manifest of idealism and common sense; and such factors as health, talents, and apostolic interests.

Such practical concerns don't deny that God might be directly inspiring a sincerely seeking person. Grace is usually granted in line with a person's unique nature, talents, and limitations. God works within the given structures of human life. We must respect these structures, which are his creation, and discern how grace builds upon them.

A school administrator, for example, looks at a position to be filled in the light of the needs of the students, the existing faculty, the goals of the school, and its educational philosophy before interviewing applicants for the job. He or she considers each one against the background of this particular situation and only then selects the person who seems most compatible with the future of the school.

Like the administrator, the vocation counselor looks at the person and the situation in the interest of reaching the wisest decision. She's aware that the appeal to concretize one's life call in some vocational form (married or celibate) comes from God and that it usually ties in with what is humanly possible in the person's here-and-now life situation.

What counts most is the person's desire for intimacy with God, for living in the solitude, silence, prayer, and reflection that ready that person for and enliven this personal relationship. Next in line of importance is the physical, mental, and psychological stability of the person. Standing on such a solid foundation, he or she will be able to radiate a life of intimacy with Christ in the culture — in classroom or kitchen, office or parish setting.

Another decision concerns the form in which to make specific the inmost call a person receives. Is it to be in marriage or the single life? As a parish priest or through celibate sharing in a religious community?

A vocation counselor might not be able to answer all of these questions, but she can help someone to assess her situation at present as well as prior to her desire to make a deeper commitment. For instance, if a woman wants to become a religious, a sufficient pre-entrance period will help her to see whether there are any major points of incompatibility between her present life and the life she will be leading as a sister. At the end of the pre-entrance period, she prayerfully makes her decision — knowing that she's still dealing with the deepest of questions.

There's always an element of uncertainty, of sheer mystery, in regard to our life call. For instance, if I desire to become a concert pianist, I have to find in myself not only a minimum of talent but also the willingness to devote myself to the discipline of practice and study. There would be in me a spontaneous turning from other involvements toward those concerning music. If my playing consistently lacked life and understanding, if I rarely came prepared for lessons, if I showed annoyance at the slightest criticism, I'd begin to wonder what "voice" I heard when I spoke of my desire to become a virtuoso.

Is my listening in tune with my life situation? Am I in touch with my gifts and my limits? Is there a strong enough desire in me to make the ideal of becoming a concert pianist a reality? Was the thought of fame simply an interesting fantasy I perpetuated about myself? What are the real motivations behind this professional "call"?

To find my vocation, I must search for signs in my present life that seem to point to it. For example, how consistent is a person's desire to enter religious life with the way in which he or she lives in the world? There should certainly be evidence of an attraction to prayer, reflective living, and selfless service. Minor differences can be worked through, but major ones might be irreconcilable with the aims and limits of religious life, despite what seems to be a person's "calling."

At the Last Supper Christ addressed these words to his disciples: "You did not choose me, but I chose you, and appointed you that you should go and bear fruit . . ." (John 15:16). The question of who is destined for one or the other vocation and who is not is definitely the work of the Spirit. How a person responds to that call depends on his or her unique character and personality and the needs of the community he or she intends to serve.

What is central in any life call is the invitation to personal holiness in the Lord; what is secondary is how this call is to be made concrete.

My eagerness to listen to a specific call might blind me to my own limitations; hence it's always wise to find someone who can widen my view and address sides of my personhood I don't see myself.

We're often poor judges of our own situation; someone trained in vocational guidance can help us to see whether our call is from God or simply a self-willed option — that is to say, one I have chosen and am determined to pursue under any circumstances.

The person whose guidance I seek enables me to understand and evaluate what is central in my life. He or she assists me in discovering whether I'm truly called to be married or to pursue a celibate life in the world or in a religious community, and further, whether I'm oriented by talent and interest to this or that professional commitment.

Because of this person's wisdom, learning, and life experience, he or she is usually able to look at all sides of the situation in a more objective way. The person's responsibility is to invite me to discern, pray, observe, and discuss what's best for me, keeping in mind the variety of channels in which God might call me to fulfill his loving plan for my life.

3

In Need of Spiritual Direction

Is spiritual direction a necessity to deepen religious living?
What can we do if we want a spiritual director but can't find one?

When I journey to a place I've never been to, I seek the best direction. I read maps, talk to people who have been there already, arrange for places where I can stop for food and rest. Once on the road, I trust that the directions mapped out for me are correct.

It's possible to apply the same criteria to spiritual direction — namely, to seek help from an expert to guide me to my divinely willed destination. The wise traveler gets directions before setting out on a journey. Similarly, help is needed in religious living, especially in the beginning stages, but the need doesn't stop there.

I might feel uncertain once I'm on the road. Signposts along the way might have been changed or removed, so the chances of getting lost remain. I'd like to find an experienced guide who's able to give me directions, but such a person isn't easily located. More often than not, I must simply move on slowly but steadily, opening myself to such available sources of information and inspiration as spiritual books, conferences, worship services, and scripture readings.

Ultimately, all direction must flow from the Divine Director, Christ himself. He chose to travel with us on this journey through life to the Kingdom to come. Daily communication with him through prayer and meditation is the surest means of finding and maintaining the spiritual direction of our lives.

Jesus himself has said, "I will not leave you desolate; I will come to you. . . . The Counselor, the Holy Spirit, whom the Father will send in my name, he will teach you all things and bring to your remembrance all I have said to you. Peace I leave with you; my peace I give to you; not as the world gives do I give to you. Let not your hearts be troubled, neither let them be afraid" (John 14:18, 26-27).

These words spoken to the Apostles at the Last Supper are meant to comfort all of us who want to live a spiritual life. They call attention to the essentials of faith that we tend to forget in our day-to-day involvements in the world.

The influence of today's work-oriented society might hinder our efforts to live in union with God. We might be among the countless souls who are trying, despite many obstacles, to lead a spiritual life and who seek wise, learned, and experienced persons blessed by God with the special grace of giving them direction either in private or in a group.

The fact that these experts are few in number doesn't falsify Christ's promise not to leave us orphans. He sends his Spirit to guide and direct the people of God through the Church. He told his disciples that he would not be with them in the same way as he had been there in the past. He still assures them that they won't be alone, that the Holy Spirit will direct them, telling them what to say and do when the time comes. He also promises them peace — not the world's kind of peace, that is, a sureness we can measure; not the security of having a clear plan of how to form his Church, but the promise of hearts that need not be troubled or afraid.

In Need of Spiritual Direction

Like the early Apostles, I too keep looking for human assurance and security. I want to know how far along I am on my spiritual journey. Even if expert guidance isn't part of God's plan for me, I can trust in the direction I will receive from the Advocate sent by Christ. I can find and follow his will in the details of my life situation, in the words of the people with whom I live and work, in the large and small events of my life, in the things that surround me.

The Spirit of Jesus as Master Director might include among these people, at a particular time in my life, the presence of a single individual to help me along. This is Christ's doing, his design, an expression of his constant and faithful direction of me and my life.

After giving them his promise of peace, Christ tells his disciples not to worry, not to be afraid. He speaks these words to me as well. As an ordinary person, I join countless others who are trying, with God's grace, to be responsive to his general, loving direction. Although I might never receive the blessing of a personal spiritual director, I can trust in the Spirit's guidance to illumine my attempts.

Growth in the life of the spirit entails dying to self as center and surrendering our life more completely into God's hands. Spiritual directors focus their attention on the Holy Spirit, hidden in the depths of the soul and at work in daily life. They help us to recognize and follow the inspirations of grace so that we may be able to discern what God's will is for us as unique individuals in this specific situation.

A good spiritual director aims to awaken insights that will enable me to live in trust and surrender to Christ and not to grow overly dependent on my director.

Knowing that Christ is my permanent director, I needn't worry if I find myself without a competent guide. Christ may speak to me whether or not I have an experienced mentor at my side. If I'm fortunate enough to know such a person, he or she might lead me through the ways of ascetical practice that enable me to empty myself so that the love of God may suffuse my whole life. Through solitude and personal prayer, I learn to converse intimately with God. I also encounter him in the common ways of liturgy, word, and sacrament.

Following these ways doesn't automatically make me a spiritual person, for intimacy with God is an infused gift of grace. I can only ready myself for this gift through these means. Readiness is marked by ardent faith and a deep hunger for the word of God. It also implies silencing the desires of my undisciplined vital and ego self and listen to the promptings of the Holy Spirit in my human spirit and in my life situation.

This kind of listening is sustained by a disciplined presence to the words of scripture, the texts of the liturgy, and the writings of the spiritual masters. I have to put on the mind of one willing to be taught. I have to be docile to be a disciple. Patiently and carefully, I establish a relationship with the word by dwelling meditatively on what evokes a response in me — not grasping avidly for new knowledge as such, but seeking to appropriate God's message for my personal and social life.

When deepening of my spiritual life takes place, it does so within my waiting heart. The bestowal of grace isn't a group experience but a solitary gift given in keeping with my unique nature. The central focus of my life is my presence to God in Christ. This union of likeness is my lifelong pursuit. Since I might not have access to a person who can assist me in my spiritual unfolding, I have to be open to the broader spectrum of spiritual direction that's available in the example of other people, in talks, tapes, and writings. The absence of a personal director calls for more initiative on my part and a disposition of relative independence.

In Need of Spiritual Direction

The one-to-one encounter between master and disciple soon widens to include other relationships. From our meetings with parents, teachers, and texts, we learn more about how to pray and participate as Christians in our society. Spiritual conferences and sermons teach us what it means to follow Christ. To avail ourselves of these occasions for spiritual direction outside of a one-to-one relationship, we must adopt certain attitudes. We must try to be open to whatever a teacher or an author says that resonates within us. Soon we might experience the companionship and confirmation that come from listening to others who have followed the same road.

Think of a fisherman's son who's learning his father's trade. He's directed by the elder man, who warns him about the currents here, the shallows there, the signs in the sky that say seek shelter. Along with the wise counsel of his father, the young fisherman learns from personal experience about his own strength at the oar, how, in rough seas and calm, to know when he's rightly oriented and when he's off course. As he becomes an experienced fisherman, he'll tell you that there are "roads" on the sea as clearly marked as roadways on the land.

The young fisherman is like a disciple setting out to deepen the spiritual dimension of his life. In the beginning, he must find another or others who know the course — that is, those who know not just about prayer, reflection, and the obstacles to spiritual living, but who can speak of these experiences from the inside — just as the old fisherman can point to the treacherous rocks and concealed sandbanks that threaten to wreck his boat.

The disciple soon becomes sensitive to texts that touch his soul and direct him as surely as if they were a personal director. Because these texts address the universal conditions of spiritual deepening, he finds in them personal lights that guide his life. The danger to be watched is that he merely reads these books, as it were, on shore, where he learns a lot about boating without ever putting out to sea.

To man my own boat, I must learn to reflect on my life alone and in dialogue with the teaching Church. One way of doing this is to keep a log or journal. To become aware of how I respond to situations helps me to stay in touch with my feelings, both noticeable and less noticeable ones, and to assess their spiritual dimensions.

Writing is an aid to self-direction, since expression helps me to become more aware of the meaning of my experiences. As this inner sense of direction gains in clarity, I learn to go where the mystery leads me, with or without the help of a personal director. As fishermen have stars or other landmarks to follow, so I discover from my journal of readings and personal reflections tried and trusted rules to travel by. In writing, I cultivate that inner compass of the spirit, which, if guided by the Holy Spirit, will find its way to God.

4

Calming Down to Deepen Spiritual Life

*Excessive tension is a signal that I have to
calm down. A calmer life is generally good for you;
is it also a sign of deepening in the spiritual life?*

One morning, for no apparent reason, I might find myself
somewhat anxious and tense. Strange — I know of nothing that's
upsetting me, yet a slight headache persists along with tension in
my stomach, clammy hands, and a stiff neck. What's going on? I
mentally relive the last few days and come to the conclusion that
I've been overly pressured, neglectful of prayer, and too sensitive
to criticism. Many causes of tension have been piling up. I realize I
have to calm down, admit these anxious feelings, and find their
possible source. Only then can I feel at ease with myself, others,
and God.

The way of coming to active calm begins with my awareness
of tension. After acknowledging that I'm tense, I attempt to get
in touch with the physical symptoms of stiff muscles and a slight
headache. As this reflection deepens, I seek the cause of my tension — for instance, too much pressure. I let these feelings come
to the surface and quietly befriend them.

Am I Living a Spiritual Life?

As I try to understand my anxiety, I might get caught in an isolated concentration on self. Focusing on myself for the sake of rooting out these unpleasant feelings might make me at first more anxious and disappointed in my progress. I seem to become more, not less, tense.

This reflective approach doesn't take away the tension; rather it aims to integrate it into the whole of my gifted yet limited life.

It's good to keep in mind that tension in itself isn't undesirable. It can be a sign that my body is mobilizing itself to cope with an emergency. Tension isn't appropriate when it becomes the usual mode in which I respond to my day. A basic attitude of calm is always helpful if I want to live a spiritual life.

What can I do when I discover that my stance is stressful and often marked by tension? Merely telling myself to calm down is at best a temporary, not a lasting or effective, solution. Unless I get to the source of my tension and deal with that, I can't hope to grow in an attitude of true calm.

Reflection on my tensions might point to a resistance to some side of my life that threatens to interfere with my projects, plans, or expectations. Such resistance is often expressed in an "if only" attitude. "If only my boss would see things my way . . ." "If only I didn't have that person to contend with . . ." A litany of "if onlys" prevents me from facing up to the reality of everyday living.

One means of growing in active calm is to cultivate a loving acceptance of the persons, events, and things that enter unplanned or undesired into my life. Through prayer and recollected presence I'm able to surrender slowly but surely to the reality God allows. I can, in the words of C. S. Lewis, rejoice in its being so magnificently what it is. To attain this contemplative attitude implies that I also accept the uncomfortable tensions that will most be with me all of my life.

If I'm mowing the lawn, I have to make sure that the grass is cleared of sticks and stones. The same is true in life. I have to try to clear away the obstacles that interfere with my attaining equanimity and begin to practice this gentling experience through calming my whole self, both mentally and physically.

A good way to begin is to allow myself to let go of all that interferes with my living in a more relaxed way. I take note of my bodily posture throughout the day. Do I sit with fists clenched? Do I grind my teeth? Do I stand or sit with my arms folded tightly across my chest? When I'm listening to someone speak, or sitting alone in my room, am I in constant motion, frequently changing the position of my body? Do I feel I have to be on the go all the time?

If I answer yes to any of these questions, I might have to make an effort to relax. When I find myself clenching my fists tightly, I can clench them even more tightly and then consciously loosen them. Rather than standing rigidly with my arms crossed, I can allow them to hang limply by my side. In listening to others speak, I can try to sit still and be attentive to them. Just to sit and do nothing for a few minutes each day might also help me to calm down.

Active calm doesn't come all at once. Many of us are constantly on the move. We don't know how to say no to others. What if we did? Would the whole system collapse if we were to sit down for a moment? Some tasks are our responsibility, but there are many more in which we become involved without knowing why. We can't seem to let go and learn to take it easy.

A helpful exercise might be to look at my life and write down all the things I have to do and, beside each item, the reasons I have to do it. In taking inventory, I'll see that there are many things I do that aren't as necessary as I had thought they were. Once I realize this, I have to let them go and resolve to put this intention into practice.

Am I Living a Spiritual Life?

Being gentle and at ease can only come about slowly with God's grace and my own willingness to be conditioned by these acts of divine generosity.

When I'm more tense than necessary, I might notice that my vision narrows. I'm unable to see what's really around me. When my head is bent intently over my books, my world becomes as small as the desk in front of me. I don't see any farther than that.

When I'm worried about a particular person's response to something I've said, that person might be the only one I see out of a whole group. Other people might just as well not be there. I see only the one from whom I expect opposition. When I'm anxiously awaiting a certain letter from home, my other mail hardly affects me at all. My vision is narrowed, in each case, by my tense attitude. I'm not present to anything beyond my immediate concern.

Calming down is facilitated by exercising my natural capacity to actually see what's around me. I must slow down, drink in what is there, and take a fresh look at my surroundings.

If I'm beginning to live a spiritual life, I'm becoming aware of my own existence as that of a restless heart reaching for the Infinite. It seems as if our lifelong condition in this world is a tension, a stretching forward to touch the unattainable.

As the food of God's word increases the hunger we feel for him, we pray that we may become one of those whom Jesus calls his own.

An awareness of the infinite horizon opening all around me might terrify me instead of drawing me beyond myself. I try to distract myself from the truth, to obliterate the conscious thought of this call of the Infinite, but the strain of resistance makes me all the more ill at ease.

My own refusal of the Spirit is perhaps the deepest source of the tension that afflicts me. It obscures the vision of eternity. The defenses I've built against the mysterious Other run so deep, they're so much a part of my way of life, that I can't break free of their domination.

To experience ego desperation is to know that it's only the touch of God's hand that can make the chains fall from my wrists. Without God's help, my attempts to calm down the resistances that block the call to inner freedom are futile.

I can experiment on the level of my human spirit with techniques of breath control and muscle relaxation; I can regulate my diet and increase my physical exercise and rest periods; I can discover ways of distancing myself from business concerns without neglecting my duties; I can seek out moments of solitude and silence in which to open myself in contemplation to the presence of God.

Noble and worthwhile as these efforts are, conducive as they are to quiet, they don't of themselves produce the tranquility of spirit I seek. I must still acknowledge my helplessness before the Lord. The gentleness and peace in which I long to live must ultimately be found in utter surrender to him alone.

5

Growing in Inner Silence

Silence is an essential component of the spiritual life,
yet many complain they can't experience it either
inwardly or outwardly. There's little we can do to change our
noise-polluted world, but can we develop interior silence?

The increased noise levels of modern life are inevitable, but what we hear around us should not camouflage our restless spirits or distract us from the sense of alienation that accompanies accelerated change. Living with the roar of buses and subways, drills ripping up concrete, fire and police sirens, unwanted background music, and information overload has brought us to an acute awareness of noise pollution. To cope with this cacophony, we need to set aside times of intentional quiet. Silence is not only an essential component of the spiritual life we must preserve if we want to welcome God's word; it is that which preserves us.

What is silence? To be silent is not merely to be mute. Spiritual silence is an emptying of self to make room for God. Ultimately it is only silence that can open us to a deeper experience of God.

How do we achieve this state of silence? It is a matter of patiently letting go of our controlling, ego-ridden, manipulating selves. Willful forcing only causes more tension. Most of us have spent a lifetime focusing so intently on our projects that we can't expect to break their grip on our souls in an instant. We are like a westerner trying to learn the art of archery from a Zen master while not being able to relinquish his desire to hit the bull's-eye.

With perseverance and God"s grace, our silence will lead us to that solitude which Franz Kafka wrote about in *The Great Wall of China*:

> You do not need to leave your room. Remain sitting at your table and listen. Do not even listen, simply wait. Do not even wait, be quite still and solitary. The world will freely offer itself to you to be unmasked, it has no choice, it will roll in ecstasy at your feet.

At this point of emptiness we can turn to God, who is waiting for us in the silence. This still point is found only in surrender, in daily dying, in letting go of our ego projects as ultimate. At the center of this solitude, we may experience a oneness with the mystery in and around us.

Each time we retreat to a corner of silence in our project-oriented world, each time we practice surrender, we put ourselves in a state of peaceful readiness. We become docile. We come to know what T. S. Eliot meant when he wrote in *Four Quartets*:

> *I said to my soul, be still, and let the dark come upon you*
> *Which shall be the darkness of God.*

He concludes the poem with this reminder:

> *Quick now, here now, always —*
> *A condition of complete simplicity*
> *(Costing not less than everything).*

As we learn to cultivate these pockets of silence throughout our busy lives, we might slowly discover that action and practice are themselves being transformed into pathways of prayer. The words of Christ to the Samaritan woman come to mind in this regard:

> Woman, believe me, the hour is coming when neither on this mountain nor in Jerusalem will you worship the Father. You worship what you do not know; we worship what we know, for salvation is from the Jews. But the hour is coming, and now is, when the true worshipers will worship the Father in spirit and truth, for such the Father seeks to worship him (John 4:21-23).

We know from this and other Gospel passages that Jesus condemned the legalism of the Pharisees, whose observance of the law for its own sake was interpreted as the sole sign of fidelity to God. In these words to the woman of Samaria, Christ implies that for them the exterior *where* of worship was more important than the interior *how*. They honored the Lord with lip service, while their hearts were far from him. The inner *why* of spiritual living became blurred. In addressing the woman, Christ calls for a renewal of heart, for worship rooted in inner dispositions, not merely in cultic rituals.

No rule in and by itself alone can heighten our awareness of our personal need for silence. It's this longing that should lead us to the decision to set aside times and places of stillness in keeping with the circumstances of our lives.

Since body and soul form a unity, we can't expect to acquire inner silence without at least some discipline of outer silence. Exterior silence is meant to be at the service of interior stilling. However, it isn't wise to rely totally on external structures to enforce silence; it is the inner motivation that urges us to seek the "still point" of our soul.

What happens outside us affects what happens within. In this sense outer silence lends itself to interior quieting. Similarly, inward changes manifest themselves outwardly. In other words, the deeper our presence to the Divine, the more it affects the spiritual quality of our outer activity.

Silence is not sterile. It gives birth to communion and communication. I bring to others what I have gleaned in my quiet times with God. "What I tell you in the dark, utter in the light; and what you hear whispered, proclaim upon the housetops" (Matt. 10:27).

The best way to offset noise pollution is to cultivate an atmosphere of silence: *outer* so that I can recollect myself before God and *inner* so I can listen and respond to his word.

6

Different Approaches to the Spiritual Life

*Some people are oriented toward quiet prayer and
savoring God's word; others toward devotions and
novenas. I'm aware of the need for a flexible structure in
my spiritual exercises, but I wonder how this structure can
evolve since persons approach the life of the spirit so differently.*

Picture a sturdy tree trunk with branches of all shapes and sizes
spreading in every direction. This image depicts one solid foundation with an outgrowth of individual elements reaching beyond
the base but at the same time deeply embedded in it.

The trunk of the tree points to the basic treasury of spirituality
from which we all draw. This treasury contains the essential elements of the spiritual life, such as prayer, periods of solitude and
recollection, reading and reflecting on Holy Scripture and the
works of spiritual masters, liturgical worship, and the sacraments.
Without this foundation, there's little or no possibility for spiritual
growth as a Christian.

The structures of prayer life should be broad enough to encom-
pass these basic elements. The outgrowth of branches refers to the
personal expression of the basics as lived by each individual or by

groups of persons with like temperaments and interests. Some might find it spiritually enriching to share reflections on Holy Scripture. Others might want to express their devotion to Mary by recitation of the Rosary. Still others might prefer mainly to share in the common liturgy of the Mass and the sacraments, complemented by private prayer and spiritual reading.

We need to be deeply and personally rooted in the fundamentals of the spiritual life, aware of and respectful of the uniqueness of each individual believer and sincere seeker. Individuals, however, must not become too individualistic. As members of a faith community, we should be concerned about the spiritual growth and needs of others. If we provide room for one another to grow, we can each become the self God wants us to be.

The purpose of these structures and exercises is first to root us in the fundamentals of Christian spirituality, and, secondly, to promote the unique growth of each member within the community.

As children in a family come of age, their rooms begin to express more who they are as individual members of the family. In and through such expression, they come to increasing self-discovery. Wise parents sense this need and allow their children a certain freedom within the limits of cleanliness and good order.

Despite the fact that their rooms are different, each member of the family respects the others' preferences. All work out their preferred decor within the common elements of good taste, adequate lighting and heat, working space, and comfort.

This same freedom of expression shows up in the life of prayer. A common element such as quiet, attentive listening to God stays the same, although its expression differs. One person seems to stress the importance of contemplative dwelling upon the Word; another needs words to begin to pray and meditate. Both approaches, although different, are blessed by God. They can be combined in the same person. We often need vocal prayers to find our way to a more contemplative presence.

At times I sit still before God to taste and savor the experience of his word coming alive in me. The fullness of my being meets the fullness of Divine Reality. At other times I feel totally empty. I seem to be void of thoughts and responses — dry as dead bones. Unable to pray myself, I turn to formulated prayers and devotions, as well as bodily gestures and postures, in the hope that they will become prayers for me. Since I can't pray, I let my body and these prayers "pray for me." They become the expression of what I'm capable of offering God now.

Within our personal prayer life, we run the gamut of experience. One day we need only to listen to feel spiritually enriched; the next we need formulated prayers and devotions. Whatever exercises we use, our aim is to keep alive the purpose of religious living — greater intimacy with the Divine Persons.

We have to be attuned to what's best for us spiritually today and courageous enough to seek it with diligence and docility. It would be wonderful to hear and heed the word of God every time we pray, but each day we bring with us different joys and sufferings. Attentiveness as well as tiredness, lightheartedness as well as lethargy accompany us along the way. By being present where we are and to what we feel, we can become flexible enough to find and follow those exercises that best deepen our presence to God.

The same can be said for our life in community. All of us are at different places on the spectrum of life experience. Because of these differences, a flexible structure of spiritual exercises is essential. Integrity teaches us to appreciate the importance of flexibility within every faith community. No one exercise can answer the needs of all at a given moment; a number of options are necessary.

Am I Living a Spiritual Life?

The point on which we most need to focus has to do with those structures that are essential. If we look at the rules required by the founders of religious congregations, we see that the founders' concerns centered on a few basic principles: the need for prayer, silence, spiritual reading, retreat, and always the practice of charity. Through the years members might have added special devotions and favorite exercises to the original customs and practices — all of which helped to nourish the spiritual lives of religious but none of which were seen as absolutely essential.

Time for prayer isn't negotiable, but a special prayer to a favored saint is. Such prayers might be inspirational for the persons saying them, but they're not so basic that everyone in the community has to adopt the same devotion.

One person might be most aware of God's presence while sitting quietly in the chapel; another might find that she has a sense of identity with Christ while making the Way of the Cross. What proves to be a distraction for me might be an ideal exercise for you. The point is: both of us are praying. There's no need for one to adopt blindly the other's devotions.

A problem arises when this individual approach leads to a neglect of the fundamentals. For example, attendance at Mass and prescribed community prayers might be neglected in favor of making a special novena or participating in a prayer group. As long as caution is exercised in regard to essential conditions and community exercises, it's wise to respect the uniqueness of each person's life of prayer and participation.

What speaks to us in a scripture passage might not touch someone else. Our unique profile of strengths and weaknesses makes for limitless openings to prayer. This diversity is as beautiful as that seen in nature. Yet this beauty often goes unnoticed because we're too close to the forest to see the trees. Instead it becomes a source of conflict.

It might be advantageous that times and kinds of personal prayer become the responsibility of each Christian. Just as a tree blossoms at its own pace, so each person's prayer life ought to be an expression in the Lord of his or her response to the pace of grace.

To impose one form of prayer on all members of a community would lead to impoverishment, both for the individuals concerned and the community as a whole.

Jesus reminds us that there are many dwelling-places in his Father's house (cf. John 14:2). The Father doesn't expect us to fit into the same place in the same way. He has allowed for variety and diversity in all manifestations of creation. By the same token, we go toward him on our own timetable of spiritual maturation. He respects the uniqueness and commonality of our faith journey. The question is, do we?

7

Living in Reflective Meditation

Would you elaborate on the meaning of "reflective meditation"? Are there steps to the formation of this practice, especially for the priest, minister, religious, and layperson?

"I can't meditate."

"I don't know how."

"It's not for me."

How many times have we heard these familiar refrains? And yet . . . take a walk along an ocean front, and you'll find many people, young and old, sitting on the rocks doing just that — meditating. They feel the necessity to withdraw to a quiet place, to set aside a time, if possible each day, to ponder the meaning of life and the direction it appears to be taking.

This quiet place might be bedroom or basement, oceanside or mountain retreat, whatever facility is available that will foster an atmosphere of silence. Finding an outwardly silent setting is only a first step; it's necessary to grow still within, for no one can meditate when their mind is like Grand Central Station.

If our thoughts are in a frenzy, we simply won't be able to ponder reflectively. Difficult though it might be, quiet concentration and perhaps repetition of a sacred text, will lead to quietness of mind. Although distractions might disrupt the surface, deep within we'll experience calm waters. Gradually we leave behind the outer tumult and open our hearts to the words of the Father.

Meditation won't solve our problems; it won't free us from the monotony of daily chores or make our bad habits disappear all at once. It will help us to face each new day with renewed faith and vigor. In a time of decision, it will encourage us to discover who we are and to discern what God is asking of us. If we're able to reflect on the words of the Gospel in a meditative way, we'll hear more personally Christ's message of mercy, his promise of forgiveness.

Meditative reflection unites our mind and heart to God; even if we're alone in a quiet place, we're at one with him. The nearer we are to the mystery in meditation, the closer we grow to one another. We learn the true meaning of life and love.

In meditative reflection we see our whole self as made in the image and likeness of God. By contrast, if we isolate a particular emotion, motive, or need, without seeing it in a wider perspective, we might get caught in introspection and begin to identify who we are with only these limited aspects of our being. Meditative reflection admits the whole picture, introspection merely a part of it; introspection isolates only certain attitudes and responses as worthy of our attention and ignores the rest.

The soil in which it's rooted gives the flower the stamina to withstand the forces of nature. Likewise if I look at myself as rooted in the sacred, I see that it is God alone who gives me strength. It is he who sustains my being and gives me life. If I cut myself off from the mystery in introspective isolation, I lose touch with the healing presence that is my hope.

Because I'm human, I will fall; because I've been redeemed, I'm able to rise again. The joy of the Christian life is that we can be and become our best self. Behind everything that happens to us, we try to see in faith a loving Father, who cares for us at every moment, who heals our past and transforms our future.

The incentive for living a life of meditative reflection must stem from the conviction that all that is points to signs of divine wisdom and truth that both reveal and conceal our calling. In meditation we open our hearts to this revelation in a more conscious way.

We might prepare for meditation by trying to focus our attention on something as mundane as the way we handle a simple daily chore. I can, for example, try to pick things up and lay them down, attentive to my attitudes. Am I sensitive and reverent in my actions or grasping and unfeeling? Can I modify my approach and spiritualize such chores spontaneously?

What happens in this example of attentiveness to how I use my hands can be applied to all events of life. I can see them as revelations of God's love and appreciate them as pointers to his presence. I can learn to treat the many events of my life — the persons I meet and myself too — as worthy of respect. I can open myself to receive all that is as an expression of God's generosity. Often I can't fathom the disappointments and limitations I find in myself and others, but somehow, if I believe that what occurs is part of God's direction, I might begin to behold the ups and downs of daily existence in a different light. My view isn't based on my expectations, imaginings, or desires but on the trust that all of life is under God's care.

To learn to reflect meditatively involves a gradual process that anyone can undertake. All that's required is that I regularly set aside some time to look at my situation in God's light. Slowly I begin to discover those self-centered, envious, or negative outlooks that distort my view. With God's grace I may be able to transform these obstacles into occasions for faith-deepening. I open myself to the silent meaning behind all epiphanic manifestations of the mystery.

I let go of plans, timetables, and projects, if only for a few moments. The words of the *Magnificat* come to mind: "The Lord has done marvels for me. Holy is his name" (cf. Luke 1:49). Whether I'm a priest, a minister, a religious or a layperson, I can quietly ask what are the "marvels" God has done in my life? In what ways has my Beloved manifested his concern for me?

He has granted me the knowledge of himself.

He has opened my heart to his divine presence,
allowing me the joy of his peace.

He has eased my burdens with his yoke,
giving me gentle lessons on how I'm to
live my life with love in surrender to his will.

He has stilled my anxious worries.

He has comforted me in times of loss and pain.

He has made me aware of my relation to all creation.

He has given me a sense of my infinite worth.

He has graced me with abundant life.

8

Spiritual Reading and Presence to God

How much time should I spend on the discipline of spiritual reading to make it fruitful? Does this reading affect my consciousness of God's indwelling presence throughout the day?

A new awareness of the graciousness of God often threads its way through the day if we are faithful to the practice of spiritual reading. Even if we can spend only a minimum amount of time on this exercise, it can enable ordinary life to blossom with a host of new meanings.

The possibility of experiencing the touch of God in daily tasks increases in accordance with the time we spend in spiritual reading. It seems to be the candle lighting up the dim corners of the portions of our day that get so busy that we forget God.

The complaint of not having enough time to do spiritual reading might be traceable to an inability to put each aspect of life in its proper perspective. If my primary commitment is the love of God, then I'll take time to imbibe his word. Professional life is important, but what about all the extras that get added to it? When I look over my day, I find there's time to do spiritual reading, provided I use my time to its best advantage.

Am I Living a Spiritual Life?

I might decide that I will spend fifteen minutes daily on the formative reading of Holy Scripture. Besides this, I might be able to set aside three half-hour periods during the week to dwell in a reflective fashion on other inspiring texts. This decision takes discipline and perseverance. If I do it only when I have the time, many days might go by without my accomplishing any spiritual reading at all. On the other hand, if I have set aside time and place for this practice, I'm more likely to stick to it. There might be a few days when it isn't possible to follow my ideal schedule, but in due time they'll become the exception rather than the rule.

Because we have trouble quieting ourselves after other occupations, we have to be prepared to spend part of our spiritual-reading time on the process of patiently slowing down our preoccupied minds so that we can be as fully present to the message of God as possible. If our minds aren't quieted, distractions will tug at our attention despite our best efforts to diminish them.

The conviction that we need a certain length of time to do spiritual reading is beneficial, but it shouldn't make us scorn the five or ten minutes of the day we sometimes find are all that we have left for God. Although we shouldn't presume on God's generosity and indulgence, we mustn't forget that the Spirit is capable of illuminating some bland word or trite maxim so that our spirits are transformed in a brief moment of genuine attention.

If professional life doesn't seem to allow us to spend as long as we'd like on spiritual reading, there are several questions we might ask ourselves. Is it true that we can't give more time to it, or are we placing exaggerated importance on certain aspects of our work?

Is what we consider a minimal amount of time really adequate to meet our spiritual needs? Compare the case of a busy wife, who, while availing herself of daily moments for genuine communication with her husband, has to look forward to the weekend or the holidays to satisfy her heart's desire for a long, unhurried time of togetherness.

The intensity of professional life ebbs and flows. There are always portions of the day when we're less busy. If we can build into our schedule at least short periods for slowed-down reading, we'll have received our "daily bread." Then we can always devote more time to spiritual nourishment when occasions such as a day of retreat come along.

The fruits of God's self-communication that come to us in spiritual reading remain long after we have received them; they make us more sensitive to his communications in other aspects of our life.

The urge to deepen our spiritual life by paying more attention to such reading can be dismissed in the rush of daily activity. People, problems, and plans might preoccupy us, but this call, however faint and transitory, is an invitation we owe to ourselves to take seriously.

To let whatever time I spend in reading become an expression of God's will for me and to experience this grace, I must be convinced that here is where God wants me to be at the present moment. Here is where his grace will exert its mysterious power, revealing to me the true Christ-form that hides beneath the surface of my anxious cares and concerns.

This period of reading acts as a bridge between public presence and private prayer. Most of us have experienced the impossibility of moving directly from intense work into relaxed worship. We realize that spiritual reading helps to still our minds and creates an atmosphere of awe.

Through this style of reading I'm able to discover again my inner center, often smothered amidst the noise and distractions of the everyday world. Letting myself be touched by God's word is like turning my face toward the wind and feeling its gentle force against my skin. It's like stretching out on a sandy beach and allowing the rays of the sun to penetrate my chilled body.

When I approach the Word in an attitude of relaxed receptivity, it's able to spiral into the core of my being. It touches me gently yet firmly and makes me aware of those areas of my life that need to be warmed by God's light. Spiritual reading helps me to see more clearly who I am before God, to realize how rich my life becomes when I allow myself to depend solely on the grace that sustains me.

God might use the power of the word to draw me more closely to the heart of love by deepening my longings for union and communion. I begin to sense the direction God wants me to take and the way I'm to respond.

Spiritual reading, like an encounter with a friend, is full of mystery and surprises. It's unpredictable in its demands and its revelations. Just as I can't know in advance what to expect when meeting a friend, so I don't know beforehand how and where the Holy Spirit will lead my human spirit through an encounter with holy words.

Such reading might affect me the way rest does an exhausted worker. It might bring to my tired body and soul a slow, imperceptible healing. The amount of time I devote to this practice isn't as important as the attention I bring to it. If I'm able to spend even a few minutes each day in quiet recollection and attentiveness to God's word, its effects will undoubtedly bear lasting fruit in my life.

9

Formative Scripture Reading

I'd like to know more about formative scripture reading as a means of contemplating the mystery of our Faith. My tendency is to analyze scripture to the point where I neglect the humility of listening. Would you please comment on these aspects of spiritual reading?

When geologists search for oil, it's important to target the exact place where "black gold" may be found. Merely to locate its source isn't yet to enjoy its benefits in our lives. A second phase has to be entered into: the "drilling" stage. A spiraling drill starts to bore into the exact location; it goes deeper and deeper each day until, slowly but surely, the hidden treasure gushes forth.

This description tells us something about how to read scripture. On the one hand, we try to gain precise exegetical information by the use of our analytical intelligence. On the other hand, we try to obtain such information outside the time we reserve for the formative reading of scripture. We entrust the former phase of our search to the enlightenment of the Church as we attempt to locate the doctrinal limits within which the revealed scriptures can be experienced, elaborated upon, and applied to our daily lives.

Am I Living a Spiritual Life?

A spiritual or formative approach to reading scripture focuses on a prayerful, spiraling penetration of the text. Illumined by the gifts of the Holy Spirit, we dwell upon what we read. Our listening becomes a drilling into a delineated place and a patient waiting upon the inexhaustible treasures found in sacred words.

Spiritual reading of scripture drills for the mystery of God's presence in the crust of its every expression as well as in the life situations where this mystery speaks to us personally. The symbolic richness of the text can point to its meaning for us if we slow down and stay with it, letting its inner depths nourish our whole being.

An analytical reading, by contrast, is always inclined to be on the move, collecting new ideas, whereas a spiritual reading pauses repeatedly to listen to words and ideas that well up from the inmost center of our life with God.

Compare what happens when we compile notes from a class. We find the key ideas of the lecture, analyze its primary sources of information, and structure its main points; but the class material will remain at a distance from us unless we allow it to affect us personally. Now that the key ideas are outlined, we can ask ourselves: How do I see this material verified in my attitudes and relations with others? Does this presentation ring true in my experience and theirs? This stage of consideration is comparable to what happens in formative scripture reading understood as a complement to intellectual analysis.

If we get together as a group for shared scripture reading, it's helpful to clarify the aim of our session. One member might want to make his archeological and socio-political background central, whereas everyone else also wants to share the meaning these texts hold for them. Personal experience isn't to be treated as secondary to the sharing of information but as complementary to it.

As we listen to one another, we might find that we've experienced the same words of scripture in a different way due to our unique temperaments and family situations, our personal history and educational background. The variety of meanings each of us sees in scripture, the applications we make, seem endless.

Consider the passage, "Sell all that you have and distribute to the poor, and you will have treasure in heaven; and come, follow me" (Luke 18:22). For one person, "all that you have" might mean time or talent; for another, possessions; for still another, prejudiced attitudes that kept him or her closed off from others. Likewise "the poor" does not always mean the materially destitute. Aren't we all poor due to Original Sin and the need for spiritual guidance?

To find out which meanings are appropriate for my own life, I need to sit down and reflect, to allow my life and the Lord's operation in it to pass before my eyes — not to analyze this mystery out of existence but to enliven its meaning.

When a friend puts a carnation on my desk, I admire its beauty and see in it a symbol of the other's caring presence. If I were a botanist, the flower would interest me both for its beauty and as a species of a floral genus.

Both ways of looking at the flower are good, but each has a different aim. In the first instance I'm open to its mystery and to what it says to me. I let myself be captivated by its beauty rather than taking hold of it to further my knowledge. At another time, I might need to make use of my knowledge of the flower rather than standing still to admire it.

Similarly, there are moments when I want to learn what theologians and exegetes have to say about the meaning of God's word in scripture as revealed by biblical study. Later I might bring to prayer what I've discovered through learning. For example, many meanings of the story of Zaccheus (cf. Luke 19:1-10) might emerge from this background knowledge. I might reflect on the way in which the mercy of God is made manifest in the meeting of Jesus and the tax collector. At another time, I choose not to mull over in my mind all that scripture scholars have said about this incident; I remain quietly present to the mystery of God's mercy — no longer analyzing the scriptural passage but reflecting on it prayerfully. I might do so alone or with others. What they share with me during a time of formative scripture reading might lead me deeper into the mystery I'm reflecting upon.

Each approach — informative and formative — has its limitations and blessings. Perhaps our problem lies in setting them apart from one another. Instead of doing so, we should place one way in the background and then allow the other to come to the foreground.

Just as we don't look at a flower in the same way when we admire it or study it, so we need to approach scripture with a different look at different times. For instance, I set aside the analytic look when I'm involved in the look that opens me to mystery. I no longer take hold of the scripture passage; rather I allow it to take hold of me.

In prayer and reflection, I sense God's word speaking to me through my life experiences. I dwell in the atmosphere of the Spirit's transforming power. I recall the changes sacred words have effected in my life because of my personal response to scripture. I see not only its surface meanings but also the inner depths of faith made manifest in the passage at hand.

Much of what I receive from prayer depends, of course, on my preparation, just as the behind-the-scenes activity makes for a good play. As the actors must study their lines to deliver the full intensity of the dramatist's message, so too I must prepare myself to receive the gifts the Divine Word wishes to give me.

Scripture study helps to refine our sensitivity to the faith horizon of the text. Because we are spirit through and through, we are always hungering for more meaning. Our thirst for God is unquenchable.

Formative scripture reading is a definite aid in our quest for God. In this exercise we're aware that a power greater than we may ever know is at work in our lives. That power is a Person whose presence beckons us beyond what mind or heart can ultimately fathom.

The symbols and words of scripture are pointers to the person of Jesus, who wants to become one with our personhood. Through his words, read and meditated upon, we prepare the way for Christ to dwell deep within the core of our being and to touch and transform all that we are and do.

10

Keeping a Spiritual Journal

Could you comment on the keeping of a spiritual journal
as a means of slowing down to develop a deeper spiritual life?

Slowing down, especially after a hectic day, allows me to savor God's gift of life. I remember, however briefly, that this day, like all others, is his gift. I might try to relive parts of it in memory and record my feelings and failings in a spiritual journal. Writing arouses a certain self-composure and lets me slip into that peaceful readiness that awakens my spirit.

The spiritual journal itself is a means of slowing down. First I have to take the time to do it, time away from everything else. The discipline of finding quiet moments in solitude is difficult to do. My days are eaten away by many obligations. It takes a special effort to keep that appointment with my journal, but if I do it, I'll find that writing like this affects for the better the rest of my activity.

Sometimes my life seems so frantic that I feel breathless. There are classes to prepare, meetings to attend, and follow-up phone calls to make, without a break. Although physically I might still be moving from one task to the next, my tense muscles tell me that

I'm doing so under duress. Even at night, when I should be resting, I'm reliving the day's round of doings.

It's tempting to tell myself that I'm busy in the service of the Lord. In my journal I can't lie to myself. I reflect on the day, on my nervous preoccupations, on how this pace interferes with prayer. I note that praying has become only one more activity alongside others that "I have to do."

If I'm honest with myself, this kind of reflection will make me more aware of my spiritual life. Imagine stepping outside and taking a walk. The night air is fresh and cool. There's no traffic on the street. I'm alone in stillness counting the stars. The air is delicious, and I breathe deeply, noticing the cleansing fragrance of the trees and shrubs. My head clears. My whirling imagination calms down. I put aside the pressures and disappointments that keep my mind and emotions racing. These draughts of night air purge my feelings and give me some distance from my day.

Under the open sky, I enjoy a down-to earth pleasure: the sight of stars, the smell of sweet night air. I'm in touch with myself. I have the sense of being in one place and in one piece — no longer trying to sort out and keep control of dozens of factors in a daily puzzle.

I think, "Today I did it again. Concentration and control. That's all I cared about. Telephone calls and office demands. Problems, not people. I wasn't in touch with how I felt except for that one moment when I tried not to lose my temper. Admit it. Only a part of me was present today: my skill and self-control. Face it. This lack of involvement is what turns my activity into a treadmill."

Writing preserves these observations and enables me to return to them. In my journal I discover that my prayer life isn't the integral part of my day that it ought to be. "I'm Martha, busy about many things (cf. Luke 10:41), and my spiritual life suffers in the process. I want to slow down like Mary and sit with Jesus, but there's all that work to be done, all those people to be cared for. . . . Can I be indifferent to them?"

Now is the time to journal about this dilemma, to reflect on the directives it evokes, and to reorder them accordingly.

Journal-keeping isn't a mode of cool calculation. I place myself in God's presence. I see that I need to spend time in prayer before and after I write. I have to slow down if my worship is to become true worship and my work true work. Contemplation has to be the ground of action; it has to permeate all that I do.

The realization of the wisdom of slowing down to write and reflect comes with effort and practice. The spiritual journal is a means to facilitate this dwelling approach. At the same time, it's a vehicle for discovering its beneficial effects on my life as a whole.

Taking time to watch everyday events and recording what happens increases my awareness of their meaning. For example, I drop an ice cube in hot water and am captivated by the hundreds of tiny bubbles that play along the edges of the cube, making a soft sizzling sound. All of a sudden the pressure becomes so great that the ice cube flips over on its side and disappears in the water. I think about the billions of molecules interacting with each other before my eyes, and for a moment this meditation on the mystery of nature lifts me out of my ordinary routines to marvel at the greatness of God, who created everything, from the tiniest bubble to the vastness of the cosmos.

To accept such a gift when it is given, to hold on to the beauty of the moment in words, is to feel refreshed in God's presence and ready to begin the day with a new outlook. Moments like this occur more often than we think, if we take the time to notice them as an artist or poet does.

Am I Living a Spiritual Life?

Keeping a journal becomes a means of making us more conscious of our surroundings. In our performance-oriented world we tend to live either in the past or future, fretting over what was or planning on outcomes we can never predict. We lose touch with the present, with the shape and color of today's landscape. Our journal helps us focus on the here and now.

The street, which before was merely a blur, reveals an intricate way of life. I notice the expressions on the faces of the people I pass. A group of men are chatting about the ball game yesterday. A young mother tries to discipline two small children who would rather walk by themselves than take her hand. A middle-age shopper looks regretfully at her heavy parcels.

Slowing down enables me to see the world in all its splendor. Recording one message readies me to receive another. I write down in my journal memorable things that happened to me today or the reflections that are going through my mind concerning tomorrow. Writing enables me to behold everyday reality in a wiser way. I become filled with wonder at the mystery of God's working in my life. I begin to sense where the Spirit is leading me from the passages I write and reread in my journal. I see more clearly the way I must follow. I move toward the mystery that harmonizes all sides of my experience. This sense of wholeness, of coming together with myself, others, and God, is perhaps the best reward of journal keeping.

A friend once told me, "One sure reason for journaling is to know myself better. I see my journal as a kind of stethoscope listening to the pulse of who I am. It helps me to value my own spontaneous responses to life rather than those that society expects of me. It also allows me to discern more clearly my spiritual direction. When I note repeatedly that I've chosen one path over another in a given situation, I sense that this is surely a pattern of behavior I need to examine. My journal is a means through which I come to assess my situation more objectively. It has proven to be a tool for self-understanding and necessary change."

It takes conscious effort to be so candid, but the result is well worth the discipline required. A good preparation for journal-keeping is formative reading. I'm not concerned about covering a lot of material or finishing a book; more important to me is the choice of certain passages to reflect upon during my reading time. I place myself in a proper mood of stillness; then I begin to read a few passages slowly. When a phrase speaks to me, I pause and reflect on its meaning. I resist the urge to move on; I try to stay with it as long as it appeals to me.

After I've done my reading and paused to reflect, I find that there's value in writing my reflections in a spiritual journal. Putting my thoughts on paper lets me see their meaning in another perspective; it helps me to appropriate the directives I do receive.

Thomas Merton observed in his spiritual journal, *The Sign of Jonas*, "At work — writing — I am doing a little better. I mean, I am less tied up in it, more peaceful and more detached. Taking one thing at a time and going over it slowly and patiently . . . and forgetting about the other jobs that have to take their turn."

By taking one thing at a time in patient attentiveness, we will in the end accomplish much more than by our frantic running from here to there.

Once I've decided that it's necessary to slow down, I might make the mistake of trying to do so instantly. I forget that this quieter stance entails a long process; it requires time to undo bad habits. If I've been working at top speed, I can't expect to brake all of a sudden. The fact that I'm able to say to myself, "This will take time," is a first step toward "slowing down."

Am I Living a Spiritual Life?

Trying to reprogram the rhythm of my life might result at first in fitful efforts. When I'm neither working well nor praying well, I have to keep repeating to myself, "This will take time."

Being gentle in my efforts to slow down means that I respect who I am. I'm not a machine with an on-and-off button. I have to learn to wait upon God's word and to become aware of my particular pace. When I notice that my hands are clenched as I sit in the bus, I relax them. When I feel that my shoulders are tensed as I hurry to classroom or chapel, I let them drop. When I catch myself rushing from one place to another, I walk more casually.

Soon I learn to look up from my work spontaneously, to take a breath, to let my eyes go out of focus, and then to look at . . . a branch scraping against the windowpane. In these moments of detachment, I become aware of God's presence in all I see and do. I'm refreshed and ready to start again.

A major obstacle to my efforts to slow down is the "Atlas attitude" toward life. The whole weight of the world is on my shoulders. I must not slacken my pace or lessen my vigilance. I have a tremendous need to be in charge. I *must not* let down my guard.

In his *Letters from the Desert*, Carlo Carretto speaks about this sincere but deluded way of seeing:

> With this mentality I was no longer capable of taking a holiday; even during the night I felt I was "in action." . . . One raced continually from one project to another, from one meeting to another, from one city to another. Prayer was hurried, conversations frenzied, and one's heart in a turmoil.
>
> As everything depended on us . . . we were quite right to be worried.

It took Carretto twenty-five years to find out ". . . that nothing was burdening my shoulders. . . . I had been holding up absolutely nothing. The weight of the world was all on Christ Crucified."

It might take me years and years to learn the same truth. To slow down is to get in touch with this mysterious gift of God that I am. Other people's standards are not my own, so I don't have to strain after them. The journal I keep helps me to see that the Lord is my pacesetter. I need to stop and rest, lest I lose the serenity he allows to flow into my soul.

11

Spirit of Poverty

Some describe poverty as an attitude toward things. Others speak of an inner spirit of detachment. What is authentic poverty? What does poverty of spirit really mean in regard to the inner life?

Such a question might make us worry about what we do possess and enjoy. A guilty feeling could come over us. "I have so many things for my own use while so many miss what is necessary." Instantly I begin telling myself that what matters isn't that I have things but that I'm detached from them. Is this attitude fully in harmony with the spirit of poverty the Lord taught us to live? Christ became poor to enrich the lives of all people with his redemptive love. He emptied himself, but God raised him high (cf. Phil. 2:8-9).

Temporal riches can become obstacles to spiritual wealth if we're not willing to share in Jesus' mission of love of neighbor and service to others. We're not free to follow him if we're bound to our possessions in an ultimate sense.

One sign that possessions might possess us is that care for them demands the major portion of our time and energy. They become the center of our interest and concern. Throwing away the things I have or giving them to the poor doesn't seem to be the whole answer — although at times and for certain people this approach can be the right response, depending, of course, on their life situation.

There's nothing wrong with things in themselves. There's no need for me to feel guilty if I find myself using them wisely in accordance with the providential circumstances in which God has called me to live. To dress attractively and appropriately in relation to my world aren't ill-spent endeavors. Neither are efforts I make to plant a beautiful garden or to arrange tasteful furnishings. Such dedication enlarges my gratitude for God's gifts and my intention to share them with others. As long as they're received and enjoyed with a sense of good stewardship, poverty of spirit is possible.

There's no gauge that measures how much is too much or what is excessive except our attitude. As long as God is and remains the center of our life, we can say that we're possessed by him and not by our possessions. We can experience poverty of spirit. What is a luxury to one person can be a normal part of life for another.

Because we're tainted by the materialism of the present age, there's no question that, for a majority of us, the things we own can become central at one time or another. We're literally assailed with messages encouraging acquisitiveness. Thoughts of poverty on any level seem to go against the prevailing thrust of our culture. Some say the so-called "flower-child movement" grew out of a disgust with the excesses of materialism. Who among us doesn't want at times to clear our lives of the clutter caused by current fads and commercially whipped-up needs? Such detachment is an essential step toward simplicity and a God-centered life.

We should never underestimate the influence of the cultural forces around us or the vigilance of heart needed to direct ourselves to Christ and away from a seemingly accepted idolatry of power, pleasure, and possession. Again, there's no blueprint to tell us what is too much. We need to remain on guard against being swallowed up by a surfeit of things while not being afraid to enjoy them in the Lord with moderation and detachment.

The attitude of poverty can't exist in my head divorced from its expression in the rest of my life. An inner attitude must be incarnated in action if it's to be real. Christ-like presence to the Father has to embody itself concretely in day-to-day living. His attitude toward things must spill over in the way I possess or dispossess myself of them.

Take the past month. It has probably been hectic, and the days ahead don't look much calmer. I grow anxious thinking about all that I have to do. How will I ever get it done? What if something comes up that interferes with the plans I've made? What will happen if I find more things added to the list of "must items" I've already scheduled?

This is certainly not the first time such concern has overtaken me, and it will probably not be the last. I begin to ask myself how an inner attitude of poverty might clean up some of the clutter clouding my life. Perhaps a consideration of the "poverty of the present moment" might help.

God gives me this particular day. I don't know whether I'll have a tomorrow, and yesterday is already past. God gives me this singular moment. It's mine, yet I'm so busy worrying about the future that I allow the grace of the present to pass me by. I forget about the gifts that are there and worry anxiously about tomorrow. I fail to remember that God will give me the grace I need to do what I have to do.

"Poverty of the present moment" is an inner attitude of treating what we have received with respect. It also influences our outer actions. We might dream of teaching the poor, of contributing to a charitable fund, or of simplifying our lives, but such ideals can become real only if they're in tune with the present moment.

When we become aware of what is, with its limits and potentials, we might find ourselves dreaming less and doing more. We awaken from idle daydreams of solving every problem and begin to appreciate the small differences we can make in service of others.

When we live in respect for the present moment, we realize how rich it is. God has given us so much more than we expected. We're filled to the brim. Our cup overflows, and we share its contents with our brothers and sisters.

What, then, does poverty mean in practice? Can I aspire to be "poor" while having the security of a roof over my head, food on the table, a well-paying job, and a place to go when I retire? I feel grateful for these benefits, but I try not to cling to them as ultimate. If poverty means being satisfied with what I "have" in a more or less detached manner, I may in humility be able to call myself "poor."

Poverty of spirit includes more than an attitude of inner detachment from what I "have." It begins with a fundamental attitude of allowing God to be the center of my desires, the source of what I hope for as well as "have." The "I" to be satisfied becomes less central as I grow in loving surrender to him.

Once we recognize God as the source of all that is good, we can look at what we have in a new light. In authentic poverty, we realize that all we are and have is gift. We stand empty before the Father, of whose fullness we receive. Of myself I'm nothing and I own nothing. I've been called into existence and am sustained by an all-loving God. Everything to which I cling in a possessive way indicates a failure on my part to recognize that what I have has been given to me.

External poverty is one means to come to inner poverty. In accepting all that is ours as an undeserved gift, we're able to participate in the self-emptying love of our Lord, whereby the Father is glorified and others enriched.

The witness of poverty consists primarily in giving of myself rather than of my possessions. Self-giving love is more difficult to offer than dispensing alms to the needy because it demands my time and talents. It extends beyond an anonymous act of reaching into my pockets and involves me in the lives of others. There are avenues for open giving spread throughout every day. Paradoxically, in giving of myself to others, I'm the one who becomes rich.

If any person or thing stands in the way of God in my heart, I can't become poor. I need to imitate Job's attitude in the midst of suffering and privation: "Shall we receive good at the hand of God and shall we not receive evil?" (Job 2:10). God must be all in our lives — that is the essence of being poor. Being rid of idols, of extras that stand in the way of service to God and others, is the aim of spiritual poverty.

A certain fervor might prompt me to give away what I no longer need or at least to simplify my life and surroundings so that I may be freer to serve God and neighbor. If such actions don't spring from a disposition of inner detachment, they remain partial gestures.

What seems most essential, as well as most painful, is to allow myself to be stripped of subtle attachments when they've become too central. Solicitude for persons and things, however genuine, shouldn't supplant the attention and care I should direct to God alone. Only when this inner work of self-emptying is going on can I complement it by maintaining a certain outer simplicity.

When what we give away is seen mainly as a means initiated by us to improve the fate of the poor, we can erode the true meaning of Christian poverty. Our motives might be centered on improving society, not on listening to God's will. Our giving might be tainted by a subtle pride that obscures the sense of our dependence on him.

Christian poverty is a grace that lets us see signs of God's reign everywhere. We can't gain this depth of inner wisdom by our own powers alone. We shouldn't forget that poverty of spirit is a pure gift that teaches us to live in appreciation for the mercy of God beyond any merit of our own.

The image of hands held open seems to symbolize the meaning of true poverty. Open hands are ready to give and receive, to be emptied and filled. They represent humility and the awareness of our complete reliance on God, however rich or poor we might be.

12

Mortification in Modern-Day Spiritual Life

Is there a place for mortification in modern life?
Is the discipline of self-denial needed, especially
when there's so much emphasis on self-fulfillment?

⌒

There are always other things we'd rather do than discipline ourselves. For instance, discipline is needed to write an answer to this question. How much more enticing it would be to watch television, read a book, or entertain a friend. No matter what excuses we could invent, writing should win first place. The alternatives might be more appealing, but we have to put them aside for the moment. To make this choice freely implies self-denial. Surely it would be easier to turn on the television, read a book, or visit a friend, but the ministry of writing must for the moment remain our main concern. It takes extra effort to gather our thoughts, assemble our writing materials, and create an atmosphere conducive to reflection. The reward of discipline is the joy of having made a commitment to accomplish the task God asks us to do here and now.

Similar openings for mortification occur all the time. They needn't be stupendous acts of denial, separated from the flow of daily life. These self-disciplines are intertwined with our situation.

Am I Living a Spiritual Life?

Smiling kindly at someone when I have a headache, lowering the volume of my radio in consideration of a neighbor's need for quiet, and learning to be punctual are some examples.

Such actions require a sensitivity that rises above personal likes and dislikes to include others' preferences. This taking into account of others implies a sacrifice of my own concerns. Each sacrifice becomes an opportunity to follow Christ. The more present I am to the situation as an embodiment of his call to die to self and rise with him, the more occasions for self-denial will present themselves. My acceptance of them as a part of God's plan for my life frees me to respond joyfully to the demands associated with discipline and discipleship.

This positive attitude of listening goes beyond the usual negative don'ts associated with discipline. "Don't play in the rain." "Don't pick the apples before they're ripe." "Don't eat sweets before dinner."

Don't . . . Don't . . . Don't . . . Even as adults, we still cringe at that idea of discipline that forbade the most delicious moments of childhood — the feel of rain, the first apples, the sweet tastes.

Discipline was equated with being a spoilsport. It was a dull affair, a tyrant. The word itself became a rod, a whip, a halt to our gallop. Added to the ordinary resistance we feel about denial is the pervasive tendency to idolize self-fulfillment. This trend is fostered by the media's enticing us to rampant consumption with no thought of moderation. No wonder mortification and sacrifice seem so distasteful.

We want the freedom to be ourselves without restraints and burdensome structures. What does this option for unlicensed liberation mean? Do I know myself well enough to handle its enticements?

Experience teaches me a great deal about my physical self, such as the weight at which I feel best. I can refuse to acknowledge this truth and literally "eat myself out of shape," or I can listen to the dictates of my body and act according to the limits of my metabolism. Do I care enough about myself to obey the truth of my organism? If I don't, what is the reason for my refusal? Is it a dislike of discipline?

Think how appalled we'd be if our favorite artist, painting a fine landscape, suddenly began to daub his canvas at random because he became bored and disinterested. As regrettable is our refusal to follow the inner call to be our best selves. Lack of discipline, in this case, clearly retards our growth.

What does it mean to become a disciple? It means to follow a person who is the bearer of truth. To know myself as God's servant. To take into account what he wishes me to do in this world. To love my neighbor as I love myself.

A true disciple engages in the noblest of tasks: to unfold the masterpiece of God's creation — the human being fully alive. Discipline, far from being a stern taskmaster, is a gentle mode of loving dedication. It is that which draws the artist to complete his picture or the poet to devote herself untiringly to the word. The true disciple follows the way of loving surrender. Discipleship transcends willful forcing; it invites us to try again to follow the way of wisdom in spite of our failures.

Daily life is replete with limiting situations that foster the disposition of discipleship. Meetings aren't scheduled to my liking. Lazy people ask for my help. Colleagues try my patience by their petty politics. I can complain about these situations, or I can let them serve as reminders of the human condition that prompt me to become a more responsible person. As a disciple, I try to listen to the Spirit speaking in my deepest self.

Too often I'm inclined to react to situations with my surface self only. This superficiality is the result of conditioning by society.

Am I Living a Spiritual Life?

I might have been trained, for example, always to respond in sweet ways to abusive words or blatant injustice. My deepest self, enlightened by the Holy Spirit, might tell me to protest against these deformations, even if some people like me less for doing so and seem shocked and indignant. The best example we can find is the life of our Lord.

People around him, conditioned by the society of that day, would tell him to be polite when arguing with the scribes and Pharisees, to keep a dignified distance from Mary Magdalene and the Samaritan woman, to ignore the businessmen in the temple instead of throwing them out and making a spectacle of himself. In fidelity to his call, Christ had to go against the conditioning of society in these instances; he had to take a stand at odds with the worldliness of the world. My deepest self, in imitation of him, might inspire me at times to do the same, whether others laud my efforts or not.

Rushing waters, harnessed in a reservoir, become a source of energy, producing waterpower for constructive purposes. So it is, in a way, with us. We're complex beings made up of many needs, drives, emotions, and potentials. This energy needs to be channeled if it is to result in self-emergence in Christ. To consider honestly who I am and what the situation requires of me demands disciplined listening. I can then choose, in the light of God's design, what is the best way for me to combine self-denial and self-fulfillment. This choice is made not once and for all. Rather than molding the situation statically to my liking, I listen each time to the voice of the Holy Spirit speaking in it.

Although I hear the call of Christ to live in accordance with the will of the Father, I still experience being drawn in many directions simultaneously. He asks me to act, while my tired body urges me to relax. I pray that I may be more considerate of others, but then find myself being impatient. "For I do not do what I want, but I do the very thing I hate" (Rom. 7:15).

Discipline helps me to moderate these willful desires. Through daily dying to self, my scattered life becomes more integrated with spiritual values and convictions. Only when I make mortification an end in itself does it lose its power to transform my life in Christ.

Self-denial is meant to soften and smooth the rough edges of my personality, not to turn me into an athlete of asceticism. It aims at making me more mellow, gentle, and Christ-like. Lived wisely, mortification has a refining power, a channeling role, a capacity to set me free from the shackles of selfishness and sin.

The deepest meaning of discipleship comes into focus when I meditate upon the life of Jesus. His death and resurrection become the pattern I must follow. Even before that paschal event, he preached the mystery of dying in order that life might flourish. He looked at the fig tree and observed that it must be pruned so new leaves could grow (cf. Luke 13:6-9). He noted that the seed dropped into the earth must die if it is to bear fruit (cf. John 12:24). He told a young man to put aside his possessions, give them to the poor, and follow him in this new way of life (cf. Luke 18:22).

I too must become aware of what in me needs to die if my Christ-life is to be born anew. The discipline of daily dying then becomes a preparation for my ultimate surrender to death as a passageway to new life.

13

Asceticism and Spiritual Development

What need is there for asceticism in spiritual development?
What is meant by the asceticism of the gentle lifestyle?

☞

"I am the true vine, and my Father is the vinedresser. Every branch of mine that bears no fruit he takes away, and every branch that does bear fruit he prunes, that it may bear more fruit" (John 15:1-2). These words of Christ are about the wisdom of asceticism and its rightful place in our lives.

The ascetical dimension can't be lived in isolation from the invitation and inspiration of grace. The Father is the vinedresser who prunes and trims clean. He speaks to us as we are, with our individual make-up, gifts, and limits. He invites us to strip away those things that clutter our life and stifle our growth in response to our calling in Christ. Usually our yes to his invitation leads us to make many acts of faithfulness amidst the trying demands of daily life rather than fostering extraordinary feats of self-discipline.

The Father inspires us to a gentle asceticism not only through the events of daily life but also through our participation in the Church's liturgical life. The various seasons of the ecclesial year provide a balanced rhythm of death and resurrection, of deprivation and rejoicing. If we enter faithfully into the spirit of each season and its celebrations, we'll discover our own ascetical balance, recognizing what must be trimmed away and what must be kept intact so that the Christ-life can flourish in us and yield abundant fruit.

If we neglect to take into account our unique situation within the balanced rhythm of the Church's liturgical year, we risk making ascetical practices ends in themselves. Holiness then becomes a matter of how much and how frequently we deny ourselves in a disposition of self-punishment. We ignore the pace of grace and choose radical practices that we expect will grant us instant holiness. Such asceticism, rather than helping us to become more Christ-like, makes us barren branches, cut off from their life-giving source.

This fallacy of uninspired asceticism has been repudiated in the period following Vatican Council II. Certain ascetical practices, several times removed from the historical, cultural, and individual context from which they had derived their meaning, were seen as incompatible with the teachings of the Church.

For a time the word *asceticism* itself fell into disrepute, associated as it was with anachronistic customs and excessive practices. This overreaction left a void that in turn led to a malaise in the spiritual life. The present outlook appears more hopeful. There are signs that Christians have been experiencing a return to asceticism, not as an end in itself but as a means of simplifying their lives in response to the invitations of grace.

A comparison with the art of pottery-making might help us to see the need for a firm rooting of the ascetical life in the soil of daily activity.

First of all, the potter chooses the clay that exhibits the proper plasticity and texture for the vessel he wants to shape. He kneads the moist material until all the air bubbles have been forced out of it. He then centers the ball of clay on the potter's wheel. He doesn't merely throw the clay on with his hands; his whole body has to be centered, completely in balance with the wheel.

Next comes the most important phase, that of shaping the vessel, of molding the mass of clay into a cylinder by gently drawing it upward, slowly pushing on the outside while shaping from the inside. As the potter's wheel turns around and around, the fingers of the artist mold the vessel from the inside, causing it to swell at the base and narrow at the neck. This "inside work" is possible only because of the potter's steadying hand on the outside, gently working with the pressure of his fingers from the inside. Throughout the whole process the clay must remain moist, but not too moist; the fingers, too, must remain moist, lest they catch on to the clay and destroy the shape of the fragile vase that begins to emerge.

The art of shaping or being shaped into our own spiritual life is similar. We must select those few beneficial experiences that will give our lives their proper plasticity in tune with our unique destiny. Then the gentle asceticism of being drawn into the chosen vessel we were meant to be may begin. The slow, gradual push and pull of our spirituality shapes our lives from the inside as we await the work of the Master Potter, who will mold us into a vessel of exquisite beauty.

As the vessel of clay is slowly shaped by being turned over and over again, so are we being shaped by the daily, repetitive practices of silence, formative reading, meditation, prayer, contemplation, and action. These exercises provide the caring push and pull we need to direct our lives toward deeper intimacy with the Trinity, but first we must consent to the tender pressure of the Master.

St. Irenaeus[1] aptly expresses this readiness: "It is not thou who shapest God; it is God who shapest thee. If, then, thou art the work of God, await the hand of the Artist who does all things in

---

[1] St. Irenaeus (c. 125-c. 203), bishop of Lyons.

due season. Offer him thy heart soft and tractable, and keep the form in which the Artist has fashioned thee. Let thy clay be moist, lest thou grow hard and lose the imprint of his fingers."

The limits we experience in daily living offer ample openings for asceticism. While certain acts of "doing without" might be good, the genuine acceptance of our limitations seems to be the key to sound discipline. Extraordinary acts of self-denial are often flights from the ordinary tasks of day-to-day dying; they carry the danger of pride posing as humility. Engaging in spiritual athletics always includes the risk of serving our own egos and the secret desire to appear special in God's eyes.

If I tend to be hard on myself, punishing myself for not measuring up to my spiritual ideals, then I need to learn to be gentle with myself. If, by contrast, I tend to neglect the spiritual life, I must find ways to practice everyday disciplines that facilitate my growing in spiritual maturity and deeper intimacy with God.

A line of the *Desiderata* reads, "Beyond a wholesome discipline, be gentle with yourself." This statement implies that we need discipline in our lives to make us gentle yet firm — to help us become the whole and holy people we were meant to be. Beyond any doubt, we ought to be gentle with ourselves — understanding and accepting our limitations as human beings. God doesn't demand perfection of us, only that we never stop trying to love him. Can we ask more of ourselves than God asks of us? Can we seek our own perfection while ignoring the invitation to be who he wants us to be?

The gentle lifestyle lets us see ourselves in relationship to a loving God, who speaks to us words of comfort and consolation. Thus the tone of voice we use toward ourselves should echo his compassion for us. The asceticism of gentleness doesn't imply whipping ourselves into shape; rather it beckons us to become more like the God who calls us to share in his love with a light and joyful heart.

14

Play and the Spiritual Life

*Please expand on the place of playfulness
in the spiritual life as distinct from being
deadly earnest about seeking our own
perfection by not wasting a minute.*

A child's playfulness awakens the child in all of us; yet playfulness is often a missing ingredient in modern life. Ever since society began to equate time with money, an erroneous emphasis has been placed on utilizing every minute. The playful child living in me falls into sterility. The "old man" or "old woman" takes the lead. I live as if I'm an extension of my computer.

The "job of life" then has to be done efficiently, quickly, and completely. Life becomes a series of rigid demands. "I have to do this. . . . I should do that. . . . I can't waste time just being with you. . . . I'm too busy getting things done."

Can the mystery and enchantment of childhood be resurrected if such is my joyless state? Playfulness depends on how freely we open ourselves to the emergence of the gentle child in each of us. Even though our world might not encourage us in this discovery, the Gospel does:

Now they were bringing even infants to him that he might touch them; and when the disciples saw it, they rebuked them. But Jesus called them to him, saying, "Let the children come to me, and do not hinder them; for to such belongs the kingdom of God. Truly, I say to you, whoever does not receive the kingdom of God like a child shall not enter it" (Luke 18:15-17).

The invitation to spiritual childhood doesn't detract from the duty to labor in the vineyard of the Lord. Neither must useful accomplishments cancel the call to refresh and revitalize our energy in relaxation. The Church upholds this Sabbath commitment in the celebration of the Lord's Day. Numerous feasts and liturgical seasons remind us that work should be put aside while the people of God gather in a leisurely worship setting to pray and sing.

These festivals point to the fact that my salvation is in God's keeping. I can't save myself, no matter how long I work or how hard I try. Faith in God's care frees me from being overly concerned about the results of my work. Knowing that salvation is the gift of the Sacred to me, I can "waste time" periodically. Refreshed by relaxation in body and spirit, I'm ready to face the crosses of life more cheerfully.

Living this balance of labor and leisure enables me to experience the inner peace and freedom of the children of God. The following legend about John the Evangelist expresses this theme well.

One day John was playing with a partridge, which he stroked gently with his hand. A sportsman came by and expressed his astonishment at finding him at play instead of busy at work. John said to him, "I see you carry a bow. Why isn't it strung and ready to use?" The sportsman replied, "That would not do at all. If I kept it strung, it would go lax and be good for nothing." "Then," said John, "don't be surprised at what I do."

The moral here is that if we insist on keeping our nose to the grindstone, sooner or later, like the taut string on the sportsman's bow, we'll either go lax and be good for nothing, or we'll snap.

It's obvious that this legend praises play as a condition for the possibility of wholesome work. As a good in its own right, play has value, but in our work-oriented society, it's difficult to be convinced of this fact. To appreciate it at all, to say nothing of "wasting" some of our precious time in play, we need to remember that recreation can improve our capacity for original work. Once we see play as inherently productive, we may be able to relativize some of our projects without suffering any pangs of guilt. If we can give ourselves permission to relax when we feel tired, we may begin to experience play as a value in itself.

Play as a servant source of productivity highlights its restorative power. As a diversion from work, it relaxes us, restores our energy, and readies us to return to our tasks with renewed vigor. When we play, the child within us leaps forth. We close our eyes to the pile of unfinished work on our desk and take off to the mountains, the bowling lanes, the local zoo. We allow the spirit of play to play in us. The solemn doing of duty fades into the distance, and we feel carefree. We let our guard down and delight in the eucharist of everydayness.

Not only do we return from play with renewed energy and a fresh outlook; we also gain new insights into the task with which we were grappling previously. While at play, unfinished plans and scattered pieces of information had time to incubate in our minds; now they mesh like so many pieces of a jigsaw puzzle.

Once we experience how play enhances work, we might also discover some positive changes in our life as a whole. We aren't as tense and anxious as we used to be. We are less impatient with ourselves and others. We learn to drop our deadly serious attitude toward life as if we were its sole organizers. Our prayer life, too, becomes more trusting and relaxed. Play makes it easier to give ourselves over to God's care and to let the Spirit play in us.

What is work for one person might be play for another. For a symphonic artist, music is serious business; for an amateur guitar player, it's simply fun. As she takes her guitar out of its case, she lets her preoccupation with the work she has to do in other areas subside. She begins to strum her favorite tune. She switches from chord to chord playfully in no set pattern, creating her own rhythmical expressions. As she plays, she draws upon an inner treasury of feelings, moods, and thoughts of the day. Her whole life seems caught up in the music. Time stands still. It's as if thirty minutes pass in ten.

Our task-oriented society might label play a waste of time, but the opposite is true. Play frees a part of my personality that lies deeper than my ability to accomplish the tasks at hand. It offers me the gift of a time break in the life of service and obligation. It gathers my whole self together in a way that's comparable to what happens when I pray. Play helps me to realize that I don't always have to be an achiever in life; I can also be a celebrator of the simple goodness that's already there.

By making room for play in my schedule, I follow the way of Wisdom, who was by God's side, a master craftsman, delighting him day after day: ". . . I was daily his delight, rejoicing before him always, rejoicing in his inhabited world . . . " (Prov. 8:30-31).

There's no playfulness possible when we feel weighed down with worry and refuse to waste a minute. What can be more useless than a flock of sparrows pecking bread crumbs, yet our Father in heaven makes their care his personal concern (cf. Matt. 6:25-26). Instead of filling every minute, it might be good to take time off and enjoy the lush banquet of life spread out before us.

Play can facilitate this freedom to enjoy what is only if it remains truly play. Our achievement orientation might be so strong that we turn every period of leisure into a grim feat of labor. Anxious competition makes relaxation impossible. A health spa might become another arena of work where we must compulsively prove our worth. Mountain travel might deteriorate into a struggle against time, an endurance test that blinds us to the breathtaking vistas appearing everywhere we turn. If we lose our capacity for play, we're also likely to neglect contemplation or "useless" presence to the Divine.

Will the earth cease to spin on its axis if we take an hour or two to let the breeze blow through our hair? In that moment of playful surrender, we might experience the Lord at play in the universe. We let control and rigidity flow out of our system; we float toward the Father, who is waiting for us. His presence buoys us up. He urges us to cast our cares upon him, to let go of our burdens, and to trust, as children do, that the Father who created us cares for us and wants us to enjoy our days on earth as a prelude to the everlasting play of heaven.

15

Freedom and Obedience

*Please reflect on the desire for personal
freedom in the context of obedience.*

⊂

Human freedom doesn't mean doing what we want to do when we want to do it. Our freedom is always limited and situated. On the side of *freedom*, we can choose the direction our life will take. On the side of *limits*, this choice is curtailed by many factors: age, background, biological and psychological make-up, education, and the demands and disasters over which we have no control.

A man born and raised in South America isn't able to become the president of the United States. A woman who has chosen to marry must leave behind the blessings of solitude she enjoyed. We're all bound by limitations. Openness to God in the midst of them is the meaning of obedience. It's a way of listening to the spiritual potential of our life within the bonds of natural and cultural limitedness.

Negative views of obedience emerge in an ego-oriented culture that stresses independence of action and reliance on personal insight and ambition. We might find in ourselves the tendency to want life to go our way. We might see as God's will only those areas of apostolic endeavor we determine to be of most interest to us.

Am I Living a Spiritual Life?

Obedience widens our perspective. It orients our choice toward whatever fosters our growth in the spiritual life. To obey is to listen to reality and to perceive our surroundings with new clarity. We're less likely to cut ourselves off from various expressions of God's will, even if they don't link up with what we judge to be our life direction.

Personal freedom and obedience ought to complement one another. We need both aspects to temper the ego-centeredness that could easily distort our appraisal of the situation. In responding to people, events, and things, we must take a stand. Here the role of freedom is apparent. By making a choice, by taking on the responsibility it entails, we grow. If we simply float along wherever life leads us, we might never find our true place in God's plan.

To become fully human, we must remain open to reality, to what is really there. By ourselves alone we're able to perceive only a limited view. By listening to what others have to say, we can check our perspective as well as broaden it through their experience. This wider view calls forth a better, although still limited, response. Because we're free, we're able to respond personally to each situation, to discern its meaning for our life here and now.

Obedience and freedom are complementary guides to mature personal growth. It's always tempting to think of freedom as having no limits until we take a realistic view of daily living. For example, if I'm tone-deaf from birth, my condition immediately limits my freedom to choose a career as a pianist. If I feel nauseated in the presence of people who are sick, my freedom to become a good nurse is severely curtailed. My secure or shaky financial situation tells me whether I can purchase the car I see in the showroom or the one on the used lot.

Everyday experience reveals how limited I am as a human being. Every time I opt for a specific direction, I add more limits to this freedom, although, to be sure, every choice also opens up the gates to new chances. I choose to place certain restrictions on one area of my life for the purpose of intensifying another.

For example, if I choose to join a religious community, I give up many facets of life in the world for the sake of developing a style of fidelity that serves to deepen my union with God. At the same time, I open myself to a wealth of experience that those who are experts in the ways of obedience, poverty, and chastity want to share with me. Although I sacrifice a part of my personal freedom, I gain the possibility of living within the framework of religious life approved by the Church. I develop a distinct facility to demonstrate the common ways that characterize a deeper spiritual life for all who seek it.

A friend of ours began teaching elementary school in a little town in upstate Pennsylvania despite the fact that she wanted to be at the university finishing her degree. She neither liked being in a place with so little cultural stimulation, nor did she enjoy the utilitarian atmosphere she found there. How could she live happily in such circumstances when her heart longed to be elsewhere?

Until now she had simply tolerated the situation. On the surface, she presented a facade of pleasantness, but interiorly she felt bitter and negative. "I don't want to be here at all, but I need the money. . . ." She felt constrained by her limits and couldn't see beyond the misery she experienced. Couldn't there be another response to this same scene?

It begins when she acknowledges her dislike for teaching there. She neither denies this feeling nor fixates on it. She decides instead to turn it into a means of growth. She realizes how disappointed she is that her dream of getting her degree will have to be postponed. She accepts the discouragement of working with people who don't share her outlook or empathize with her hopes. She chooses to accept disappointment rather than merely tolerating her position and feeling negative toward it. She willingly yields to the whole situation with its limitations and makes the best of it. She lets all the disadvantages subside and addresses herself to the positive features. This free response of refocusing lessens her resentment. She becomes more present to the task at hand and decides that one year more or less won't interfere with her degree.

This second response illustrates the fact that freedom means choosing to accept the limited reality of the situation in which I find myself. No situation is perfect. I must take a stand toward my circumstances and develop the appreciative response that signals true maturity.

Look at Jesus, whose food and drink was to do the Father's will. In the Garden of Gethsemane, he was faced with death. What fear and discouragement must have flooded his being. Yet he freely responded to the Father: "If thou art willing, remove this cup from me; nevertheless not my will but thine be done" (Luke 22:42).

In our experience of living obedience in freedom, we're bound to meet situations in which, like Jesus, we're asked to do things that don't seem agreeable to us. Despite this response, we can choose to accept what is and search for the silver lining it holds. We can also place our choice within the wider perspective of Christ's acceptance of his Father's will even unto death.

A delicate sense of hearing is required to catch that perfect pitch of God's voice in such imperfect situations. Can we dare to hope that our ears will be so delicately attuned to the voice of God? Can we be so stilled in our desires that we long in purity of heart only to obey his will?

To listen with our minds already made up is an empty gesture. Only when we allow God's voice to release our inner freedom from the bonds of pride and willfulness can we discover in peace and joy the purpose for which we were placed on earth.

16

Spirituality and Addiction to Emotion

*Various publications refer to an addiction
to excitement, emotionalism, and sensationalism
in spirituality. What is the correct relation between
spirituality and our emotional expressions?*

The word *addiction* means "to give oneself habitually or compulsively over to" something. Drug addicts like the feeling of being high because they no longer have to face the burdens of living as ordinary human beings. They give themselves over to their addiction in an attitude of impotent passivity as opposed to fostering a healthy and potent receptivity.

Choosing an addictive existence entails giving up our possibility of taking a responsible stand toward the world around us. This lack of freedom is usually accompanied by a pervading sense of brokenness. Addicted persons can no longer stand up without the help of some physical or emotional crutch. The real self God calls forth in them, however talented or limited it might be, isn't acceptable to them, so they overlay that true self with an unreal, artificially stimulated, or inflated false self. Because they can't cope with their own uniqueness or with the otherness of the world, they attempt to fuse with some substitute for freedom. They begin to lead a life that makes them wholly dependent on whatever substance or action is exciting, stimulating, and sensational to them.

Negative influences in their personal history might make people suffering from some sort of addiction retreat passively from the world of ordinary duty and responsibility. To return to the womb and start life over again is impossible, but some people still seek the secure ambience of babyhood by surrendering blindly to a compulsion or entering into a counterfeit relationship or seeking religious exaltation as an escape from reality.

This stimulating experience can cause addicts to run away from the day-to-day commitments and challenges of life. They become passively dependent on these sources of stimulation and bitterly opposed to anyone who questions them or tries to take away whatever they're addicted to.

What relation is there between such unfree expressions of emotion and the life of the spirit? True spirituality implies basic principles, conditions, and structures, while spirituality-as-escape has connotations of lack of structure, high excitement, and feelings that are out of control. However, just as on a sailboat, the rudder and the sails work together to keep the boat on course, so it's also possible to respect our emotions and to live our spirituality as a unified whole.

The rudder on the boat is the vertical blade at the stern of the vessel used for directing, guiding, and keeping the boat from veering off course. The position of the rudder directs the boat to head into the wind, moving with it rather than against it. This position determines whether the sails will catch the wind, billow out, and cause the boat to glide over the water. Without the guiding direction of the rudder, the sails flap and wave uselessly in the wind, tossing the boat to and fro as it drifts aimlessly along, with the danger that the sails will either be torn by the wind or cause the boat to capsize.

Spirituality is analogous to the function of the rudder on a sailboat. It gives us guidelines and directives for the daily living of God's will as well as greater insight into the basic dynamics of the spiritual life. It helps us to discover who we're called to be and to stay on course.

Emotions are like the sails of the boat, affected by the wind, responding to the spirit of the times or to the Holy Spirit blowing where he wills. Our sails must be guided by the rudder; that is to say, our emotionality must be directed by our spirituality if we are to sail towards intimacy and union with the Divine.

If our emotions are allowed to run loose, flapping aimlessly in the breeze of whatever wind blows, seeking only their fulfillment rather than being at the service of a greater good, the result might be mere emotionalism, which, as Kahlil Gibran says in *The Prophet*, ". . . if unattended, is a flame that burns to its own destruction." Instead of enriching spirituality through more vibrant participation, emotion detracts us from our true destination. The sails become more important than the boat needed to complete our journey.

Just as excessive dependence on alcohol is damaging to a person's health, emotionalism — excessive dependence on emotions — is detrimental to one's spiritual life. Whether I smoke three packs of cigarettes a day or watch soap operas all afternoon, whatever I do in excess, I will more likely than not find many good reasons for it. Others' excesses are always much easier to identify than my own, which I rationalize away. I try to convince myself that it's better to smoke than to be crabby all the time; that afternoon serials are not so "far-fetched" and that "you'd be surprised at the number of intelligent people who watch them." So it's difficult to see my own excesses as excessive.

Am I Living a Spiritual Life?

We might identify as an "addict to emotionalism" only the person who demands highly emotional experiences in prayer. He might not attend Mass unless there's soothing guitar music, shared sermons, and physical demonstrations of affection. She may find liturgy dull and uninspiring when it fails to evoke a state of bliss. Such an attitude seems to equate liturgy with an emotional "high." It is by definition unrealistic and removed from the true essence of worship.

Emotionalism can take another form. Holding tenaciously to the traditional, regardless of what authoritative directives have taught us to the contrary, is as much an example of emotionalism as is the search for something sensational.

What these two forms of emotionalism have in common is a missing rational component. Refusing to consider the validity of any view but my own always implies an excessively emotional stance, regardless of how unemotional I might appear.

The fact that I don't identify myself with the "excitement addicts" doesn't mean that I'm not as prone to emotionalism as they. Whatever I cling to in an unthinking way is what makes me excessively emotional. It might be an exclusive attachment to the singing of Gregorian chant or an unwavering demand for country music at every liturgy. In each situation, I'm acting out of excessive emotion.

Religious feelings belong to the most sacred moments of our human experience. Unfortunately, our search for the sublime is misdirected by feelings that have become excessive.

I can't turn off my emotions the way I can switch off the radio or television. I might try to calm the angry feelings I experience when I hear bad news or the upsurge of excitement that is my response to good news, but I find that such volatile emotions affect me just the same. Angry or elated feelings color my interactions with others and often prevent me from listening to the situation as a whole.

When I become emotionally involved in prayer or liturgy, I might find myself becoming increasingly addicted to the "golden glow" I experience. Warm feelings might become the only trustworthy indications in my mind that my prayer is pleasing to God. I can become so reliant on these feelings that I lose sight of other facets of the spiritual life, such as aridity and the need for pure faith. This preoccupation with self makes me focus on my experience instead of on the Lord, to whom I owe my allegiance.

I forget that in searching for the emotional excitement of thunder and fire, I might fail to hear God in the "gentle breeze" (1 Kings 19:12). Emotions do have a significant role to play in my approach to God, but if they become dominant, they can hold my attention so much that prayer remains a listening to self rather than an occasion of self-giving to the Lord.

By the same token, religion should not revert to being a matter of dos and don'ts. It signifies a personal faith relationship with our loving Father, whose children we are. This simple truth of doctrine appeals not only to our intellect but also to our heart.

The words of the psalmist describe this harmonious interplay in a splendid way: "O God, thou art my God, I seek thee, my soul thirsts for thee; my flesh faints for thee, as in a dry and weary land where no water is. So I have looked upon thee in the sanctuary, beholding thy power and glory" (Ps. 63:1-2).

This prayer is the seedbed of living faith that comes to fruition in liturgical experience and communal sharing. It shows us that genuine spiritual living always requires balance. Without doctrinal knowledge, religious sensations risk becoming mere emotionalism; without religious feelings, doctrinal knowledge risks remaining abstract and divorced from life.

Am I Living a Spiritual Life?

Christ commands us to love God not with our mind or with our heart, but rather with all our heart, all our soul, all our strength, and all our mind (cf. Luke 10:27). Authentic spiritual living involves our whole self in a loving relationship with God, whom we dare to call our Father.

17

Spiritual Listlessness

What can we do when a kind of spiritual listlessness takes over, making prayer, meditative reading, and reflection on the words of scripture difficult, if not impossible? Are there any practical suggestions for overcoming the problem of listlessness, which acts as an obstacle to concentration on and dwelling with God's word?

How foolish I felt after picking up my wallet and car keys, walking to the car on my way to attend a meeting, driving along, and suddenly becoming aware that instead of going to the meeting, I had automatically driven the route I take each morning to school. The mechanical action of following my usual morning route, completely oblivious of where I should have been going, makes me wonder how this error could have happened.

I recall how "out of it" I had been at dinner, sitting there like a spectator. Other factors hit me. During a recent telephone conversation, a friend had commented on how distant I sounded.

Reflection on this experience helps me to see what happens in general when listlessness takes over. In this case I came to the awareness of my loss of spirit from performing an action automatically and finding myself on the wrong road. I felt forced to reflect on my relationships with others and with God. I discover a similar pattern in both cases. Dryness in prayer is comparable to the emptiness felt in my routine engagements.

Aware of the problem, I can now consider what is blocking the depth of my relationships with others and my intimacy with the Lord. I seem to be the victim of "too much" and "too many" projects and concerns. As a result I'm lacking in relaxed presence to the here and now. A realization of my limits is in order if I'm to admit that I can't do it all, that I have to let go of some projects to provide room for the Lord to dwell within me.

Some of us tend to increase our involvements. The longer we cling to them, the more we insist they're necessary. If we were to sit quietly and enumerate every activity of our day, then in general of our week, all the while gaining a little distance from our routine patterns of behavior, inevitably we'd discover the non-essentials. The next step is to remove them gently and to create a better rhythm of being and doing in our lives, always leaving space for the serenity that sustains prayerful presence and participation.

An important prerequisite for this refocusing is listening to our body, getting in touch with its messages. When are we most tired or most alert? Where can we go to rest in God with the fewest distractions? What's the best time and place for prayer?

Reflection upon the obstacles to our spiritual life can lead to a change of direction, but we need to pursue it in a patient, practical, and loving manner, expecting no instant cure.

We must learn to listen to listlessness and fatigue and bring them to prayer for God's healing. We come into his presence with the recognition of where we are and proceed from there. Sometimes that can mean reading God's word and waiting for its meaning to emerge. Tired as we are, we might be able to manage only a simple repetition of a single meaningful phrase.

If listlessness and fatigue persist, we must find ways to alleviate them. Any remedy tends to be individual and varies with the intensity of our courage to change. What are the causes of our lassitude? Are we trying to fit prayer time into any free moments that happen along, or are we maintaining a more disciplined approach? Is the mystery central in our lives, or have we given that place to projects or persons who demand our attention? Do we seek God's presence ceaselessly, or do we come to prayer as another duty to be addressed and then dismissed? Are we patient and persevering in the pursuit of God's will, or do we demand instant proof of our fidelity?

Such reflections enable us to identify with St. Paul's urgency to "Pray at all times in the Spirit, with all prayer and supplication. To that end keep alert with all perseverance, making supplication for all the saints, and also for me, that utterance may be given me in opening my mouth boldly to proclaim the mystery of the gospel, for which I am an ambassador in chains; that I may declare it boldly, as I ought to speak" (Eph. 6:18-20).

This text reminds us that we must desire to be in God's presence, to listen to his word with so much fervor that it lifts us out of our listlessness and lets us come before God just as we are. At such moments, the words of scripture light up with new meaning:

You will seek me and find me; when you seek me with all your heart, I will be found by you, says the Lord, and I will restore your fortunes and gather you from all the nations and all the places where I have driven you, says the Lord, and I will bring you back to the place from which I sent you into exile (Jer. 29:13-14).

With an honesty we wish to emulate, St. Thérèse of Lisieux has written:

Am I Living a Spiritual Life?

> Do not believe I am swimming in consolations; oh, no, my consolation is to have none on earth. Without showing himself, without making his voice heard, Jesus teaches me in secret; it is not by means of books, for I do not understand what I am reading. Sometimes a word comes to console me, such as this one which I received at the end of prayer. . . .[2]

Lack of consolation, perhaps accompanied by listlessness, fatigue, boredom, and aridity, are familiar companions on the spiritual journey. Even the saints had to endure them. There are many times when the spirit is willing but the body is weak and lethargic. We feel weighed down with lassitude with no end in sight.

The fathers of the desert called such spiritual fatigue *acedia*. Their remedy was to stay in their cell and stick it out. They knew that *acedia*, if it was sent by God as a purification, would disappear only when it had done its work. They weren't afraid of this sense of emptiness, this desert experience, because they believed that the Lord leads us into the desert to speak to our heart (cf. Hos. 2:14).

It's wise to remember that commitment of our will to the glory of God is more important than surface feelings of listlessness. We have to maintain a simple attentiveness to God in spite of the way we feel. Our Beloved doesn't ask us to be awake, alert, and full of inspiration every time we pray; he asks us to pray no matter how we feel. Love of God, worship in spirit and in truth, are possible in the desert because it is there that we gain in purity of heart.

Fatigue reminds us of our humanness, of our need to let God in his mercy be the master of our experience. Accepting our limits lets us grow in humility. We remember how Christ responded to

[2] St. Thérèse of Lisieux (1873-1897; Carmelite nun and Doctor known for her "Little Way" of spirituality), *Story of a Soul*, ch. 9.

others when he was tired. We see him at the well with the Samaritan woman. Exhausted as he is, he speaks kindly to her and offers her the waters of everlasting life (cf. John 4:14). He ends the mental fatigue of argumentation by holding children on his lap (cf. Luke 9:46-48). We can trust that he will help us to alleviate our tiredness if we cooperate with his grace and try candidly to discover the cause of that tiredness.

Perhaps we're feeling tense and anxious about unfinished tasks or unsolved problems. We might be working so hard on our projects that we're not eating properly or getting enough rest. There might be several reasons for our listlessness rather than just one cause. In the process of looking for ways to resolve these trials, we must also learn to accept them.

We might need additional rest and relaxation before we try to dwell on the Word. It might behoove us to choose another time for prayer and reflection — one more conducive to paying attention than when our energy level is low. As long as we accept that fatigue is present and don't ignore it, we have a chance to opt for change. It's wise to remain faithful to spiritual practices like formative reflection and prayer, while waiting for signs of recovery from listlessness that weakens our concentration and sense of purpose.

If nothing else happens, we can at least offer God the "prayer of fatigue," saying, "Here I am, Lord, tired and listless and drained as usual. I have nothing to offer you but a weary body and a woeful spirit. What I have and what I am, I give to you, O Lord, with all my heart."

God accepts the way we feel, so why can't we do the same? God loves our weary soul as much as our wakeful soul. The love that flows between us transcends our listless spirit. Even though it seems as if fatigue has penetrated every fiber of our being, we find comfort in knowing that God will not turn away from us. Listless as we may be, the Gospel tells us that the Lord found us eligible to receive a special invitation addressed to weary souls, to whom he said, "Come to me, all who labor and are heavy laden, and I will give you rest" (Matt. 11:28).

18

Loneliness and Spiritual Growth

Many people feel alone and lonely. Is loneliness an
obstacle to spiritual growth, or can it be an aid in disguise?

To answer this question, we need to make a distinction between two kinds of loneliness, one of which influences the other.
Primary loneliness is the result of our being cut off from God. It
creeps up on us when we invest all of our time and energy elsewhere. Sooner or later we experience the disappointments associated with a superficial existence that severs us from the only
abiding comfort there is: union with God. When God comes first
in our lives and encompasses us totally, there's no room for loneliness. We're filled by the gift of intimacy with the Divine.

The best relief for primary loneliness is unquestioning belief in
God. An example comes from the lives of the early Christian mar-
tyrs. They were supported not only by their faith but also by the
way in which it linked them to all of God's creation. There was no
room in their lives for loneliness because they lived in total surrender to God's presence and providence.

In our era such faith is far less prevalent. Certain insights
from the positivistic sciences have eroded the consciousness of our

connection to our Creator. We suffer from a sense of alienation. Cut off from our Divine Source, we find an anxious loneliness filtering into our lives. The further we venture from God, the deeper our loneliness and subsequent despair become.

Each of us is affected by this obstacle of alienation. Even the most devout Christian is part of this society. None of us can escape the prevailing implications of scientism and humanism, but neither can we forfeit our lifelong call to discover and rediscover in faith our certitude of God's presence in creation and of his intimate nearness to us. Whenever we let go of this divine thread, we experience the malaise of our time: loneliness.

As we turn away from God, our need for worldly goods increases. To counter the vague uneasiness we feel, we surround ourselves with empty relationships and any busy work that distracts us from our gnawing sense of incompleteness. We make success and socializing the ultimate values in our life, neglecting what really matters: our elusive spirituality. We risk becoming abandoned souls, lost in a web of self-alienation that turns us farther from God.

To find our Divine Source, we must spend some time alone in solitude. There has to be a way through the maze of conflicts and unanswered questions in which we've been wandering aimlessly. Being alone in this manner can't be equated with loneliness, since solitude reconnects us to God.

Secondary loneliness comes from withdrawal from family members, mentors, friends, and neighbors. It happens when we wall ourselves off from authentic encounters that transcend infantile dependency and allow us to be with others in respect for our mutual uniqueness. Although withdrawing from people might at times be a reaction to the draining aspect of togetherness or the meaningless din of activity that surrounds us, secondary loneliness, which is always a form of isolation, is the result. It turns us in upon ourselves in denial of our oneness in God and our need for some kind of genuine togetherness.

In primary loneliness we disobey the first part of the great commandment: to love the Lord our God with our whole heart and soul and mind. In secondary loneliness we violate the command that follows: to love our neighbor as ourselves (cf. Luke 10:27).

Basically, then, loneliness is a matter of not listening to God or not caring enough about others. It's an introspectionistic movement that erodes the meaning of our existence. We lack the generosity to reach beyond our self-preoccupation to care for someone else for Christ's sake.

There are countless ways to let go of our own ego and to touch and be touched by others. There are the disheartened to cheer, the sick to visit, and the frustrated to calm. There's always someone who needs our ear, our smile, or our compassion. It's impossible to feel lonely when we're doing something for someone else, when we go the extra mile.

We can, for instance, take the initiative to be the hostess of a family evening or to prepare a surprise party for a friend. These moments of caring pull us away from feeling sorry for ourselves. Being present to others, complimenting them on their ways of being thoughtful, trying to stop and listen to their concerns — such outgoing acts as these help us to look beyond our lonely world.

As long as we remain in the prison of our loneliness, we can't grow in the dimensions of real love, which find their roots in God. If we begin to reach out to others, they will reach out to us. We shall be like the virtuous woman in Proverbs, who "rises while it is yet night and provides. . . . She opens her hand to the poor, and reaches out her hands to the needy. . . . Strength and dignity are her clothing, and she laughs at the time to come (Prov. 31:15, 20, 25).

19

Faith and Fear of Death

I am experiencing a deep fear of death.
Is this a sign of lack of faith in God?

Fear of death is part of being alive. There is in each of us an in-nate drive to live forever. Faith in God helps us to cope with being afraid to die. Enlightened by the grace of the Holy Spirit, we can submit our fears to the redeeming love of God, who lets us see death in Jesus Christ, not as an end, but as a new beginning.

Why is it that we feel so little certitude about the most certain event in life, which is death? Faith in Christ's promise of eternal life gives us the courage we need to look upon death as if it were but a transition from night to day.

Fear of death can be the Lord's way of calling us to face our fini-tude. Faith in him gives us wings to reach beyond this life with a joy born of hope. In one sense this fear is part of our nature. In an-other sense, it has everything to do with faith in God.

A near-death experience can be the high point of our life. Imagine sitting in the backseat of a car with your eyes closed and your fists clenched, praying as hard as you can because your driver is speeding on a rainy road. You keep your eyes shut. You can't sit

ntrate on prayer. Suddenly you open your
slanting straight toward a ditch. The car is
i, go limp, and then it's over. In a few sec-
.cu up, turned on its side, and thrust into a ditch.
no screeching or thudding, not even a jostling bump.
ı he driver and you crawl out of the top of the car without a
scratch. Still you feel the panic of that moment, the cold sweat,
the shortness of breath. You were sure that this was it, and you
were terrified. Why? Was it the fear of death or of dying? Of being
mangled and torn apart? Of the suffering such a violent accident
might inflict? Was it dread of meeting the Lord on the other side
while not being ready to say goodbye to this life? Was it anxiety for
others, for your family and those dependent on your care?

All of these fears were probably present, at least implicitly, but
first and foremost is the normal human desire to cling to life as our
most precious possession. All of us hang on to the gift of life when
it's threatened. Only by an act of surrender are we able to relinquish our hold on it.

Looked at from a merely human perspective, death is a separation from all we hold dear; it might also be seen as a release from
the misery brought about by old age, sickness, or poverty. In spite
of our anxiety and fear, most of us would prefer to suffer our present ills than to launch out into what we don't know: that dimension of life from which no telecasts have been beamed back.

Faith in God overcomes this fear. As we learn to see ourselves
as the finite creatures we are, we trust our Creator to bring us to
new vistas of meaning. As we say yes to his shepherding of our lives,
we realize that we're not in ultimate control. We're more able to
relax and face the moment he calls us from one form of life to another. To the faithful person, death isn't an undesirable end but a
welcome passageway to life eternal.

Fear can either inhibit my freedom or elicit awareness of dependence on God as the only source of true liberation. Fear death might be a call to withdrawal or to conversion and radical recommitment. It doesn't necessarily bespeak a lack of faith; rather it gives me an opportunity to know myself in relation to the gift of life given to me by God.

Life is a gift to enjoy and then to be surrendered. Daily we live through sickness, pain, loneliness, disappointment — little deaths that make us aware of how little control we have over our lives. We fear letting go until we really listen to the words of Jesus: "Those who love their life lose it, and those who hate their life in this world will keep it for eternal life" (cf. John 12:25). It is only in surrender of our life to the painful uncertainty of death that we can possess it.

Since we pass only once from death to eternal life, we never get the opportunity to become familiar with it. Death is a topic shunned in most conversations, yet it remains in our thoughts more often than we mortals care to admit. What makes death so terrible that the thought of it causes us to be afraid? One reason seems to be letting go of the familiar.

Does this mean that God, who is our loving Father, can no longer be seen as one in whom we can place our faith and trust? This distrust could happen if we give in to our fears and allow them to take hold of us.

Faith in God is a free gift that we must avail ourselves of to possess it more fully. Think of the Blessed Mother. She led a life of faith, but there's no denying how much pain and suffering she endured. Each sword that pierced her heart seemed to make her a woman of stronger faith, ready to endure the sight of her dying son.

What has gone by in the past might serve as a basis to grow in faith, but the future hasn't yet been revealed to us. Faith is a virtue,

Death
my

...hy we might mistake our fears for a lack of
...ur faith and trust in God as we face the
...nar. Our faith will then sustain us, even
...r it's no longer present.

...ace of suffering and death, Christ himself shed drops of
...d and besought his Father to "remove this cup from me" (Luke 22:42). Fear of death can be seen as a sign of faith rather than as a weakness, provided we attend to the warning: "You also must be ready; for the Son of man is coming at an hour you do not expect" (Luke 12:40).

Consciously or unconsciously, the human mind can never fully free itself from its final scene. To say that fear of death is a sign of weakness would be to make cowards out of the bravest men and women in history. Just as it's true to say, "The fear of the Lord is the beginning of knowledge; fools despise wisdom and instruction" (Prov. 1:7), so a salutary fear of death is a sign of wisdom as well.

The fear of death seems to decrease as the strength of faith increases. Still, being afraid of finitude is inherent in our nature because we're not created to die but to live. Our instinct for survival makes us recoil from death. Every fiber of our body turns toward life. Our entire physiology is geared for the struggle. The separation of soul and body is an unnatural phenomenon, and no one can free himself from the dread of this parting. It's a leap in the dark from which there's no return. Only faith tells us it's a leap into the waiting arms of our Lord.

Christ has prepared a place for us in his Father's house and we must focus our attention on this promise if we wish to allay our natural fears. In Jesus alone does the fear of death give way to a leap of faith.

20

Aging and the Dark Night of Faith

The dark night that seems endless often comes when a person
is middle-aged and already experiencing stress in life. What
will help me to remain faithful when I feel like giving up?

As we move into winter, it's obvious that nature has changed her scene. Autumn has stripped the trees, and their colorful foliage is a thing of the past. The change of seasons is an integral part of nature's year. Although we often wish to hasten the dismal winter days toward spring, we realize that one season has to pass to bring about the other. So we wait patiently.

Human nature affords us the same possibility of changing the seasons that seem to be interwoven in our life cycle. In the "summers" of life, we experience exhilaration, openness, and the freedom to meet new challenges. In the "autumns" we suffer a loss or a stripping of vitality. In the "springs" we know the wholeness and growth of peace and joy. Before this time of newness and growth, there was the "winter" — a period of death and dying, or a time of struggle and suffering.

To most of us, winter seems bleak and all but dead. In actuality growth continues in hiddenness, below the soil. During the winter

ınt life withdraws to recoup its forces and to prepare for
.rust of spring.

w ... dequate reflection, we can see the same cycle of nature
exemplified in our own lives. There are stages throughout life
when we must withdraw into our inner center and let the darkness
come upon us. During middle age, life seems to lose its meaning,
and obligations become oppressive. At this time weariness often
overtakes us.

Just as we don't see what's happening below the surface during
nature's winter months, so in faith we must believe that although
he's presently unseen, God is effecting an interior growth in us.
Being at home with this mystery can help us to wait patiently and
live through the dark night that seems endless.

If we believe that this darkness is from God, we might find that
he's calling us to a deeper commitment: to shed the bleakness of
what we feel for the blessedness of who we are.

In our solitude we might discover that we're extinguishing the
light ourselves by our overly active life, by our *doing* in preference
to our *being,* by interior noise rather than silence. If we honestly
evaluate ourselves in this season of our life, we might see that the
darkness is in reality a light to see what must be changed. Then, in
God's time, he may once again bring forth within us a new spring
and a realization that ". . . lo, the winter is past, the rain is over
and gone. The flowers appear on the earth, the time of singing has
come, and the voice of the turtledove is heard in our land" (Song
of Sol. 2:11-12).

As we seek to open ourselves to deeper experiences of God's
presence, we might have to endure prolonged periods when we
feel abandoned by the one who promised to be with us always. In
the past we might have felt joy and a sense of peace when we
prayed. This experience of God's presence seemed to permeate our

whole life. We knew that God was always with us, that he truly was our rock of refuge, our loving Father. We felt as secure and content as a child who slips his hand into his parent's grasp. Consolations come because God knows that our faith isn't yet strong enough to do without them.

The time arrives when we find few, if any, "good feelings" in prayer. It feels as if God has withdrawn to a place far away from us. This is when we need "pure faith" and deep trust to believe in God's constant loving presence when there are no consolations, no sensible signs of his nearness.

In the midst of this crisis of transcendence, we might find it difficult to pray. We might feel little or no consolation from spiritual exercises such as scripture reading and meditation. The truth that God is faithful to us is the only consolation to which we can cling (cf. 1 Cor. 10:13).

Spiritual masters such as St. John of the Cross[3] assure us that through such a "dark night of the soul" God is preparing us to experience deeper, more contemplative forms of prayer. In fact, the dark night seems to be a necessary period of purification, preceding our entrance into the adulthood of the spiritual life. In a comparable manner, physical separation from our mother prepares us for a more mature relationship with her and with our whole family.

Our loving Father asks us to trust him despite this dearth of consolation. He invites us to identify with his Son on the Cross, who in his dark night of suffering prayed, "My God, my God, why hast thou forsaken me?" (Matt. 27:46). If we can echo these words of faith, we can be sure that Jesus will help us to surrender as he did

[3]St. John of the Cross (1542-1591), Spanish Carmelite, mystic, and reformer of the Carmelite Order.

while praying, "Father, into thy hands I commit my spirit" (Luke 23:46).

The bedrock of our belief is that the Father, whose Son conquered death, will raise us from our death-like dark nights and bring us to the dawn of Easter morning. In this radiant light we're illumined and transformed in God, as St. John of the Cross explains in this poetic affirmation:

> O night that has united
> The Lover with his beloved,
> Transforming the beloved in her Lover.

Our inability to understand what's happening to us is a contributing factor to every dark-night experience. We don't choose it. It falls upon us with its seemingly endless bouts of aridity. We don't see anymore; we don't know anymore. We're no longer in charge of our destiny, but we do have a choice: either to let God be God or to become more frustrated by our lack of understanding. In a dark-night experience there's no way out; there's only a way through, and that's the way of letting our intellect be purified by faith, our memory by hope, our will by love.

We find it difficult to be this detached, to feel so defenseless and alone before God in the nakedness of our small and limited being.

If we respond in trust to these experiences, sobering as they are, we might be able to sing with St. John:

> O guiding night!
> O night more lovely than the dawn!

To grow in wisdom, age, and grace before God and others is to face the truth of who we are. When we lose our illusions of unlimited strength, we grow in humility.

Self-knowledge of this intensity is always painful.
life crisis, we have to face the reality of all that we wil
all that we haven't done. Our choice is to dwell either on what
we've lost (our ego-self) or on what we've gained (our Christ-self)
and the gifts of trust and patient endurance that accompany this
call to discipleship.

Part 2

Integrating Prayer
and Participation

1

Retreat and Return to Reality

*During retreat, the divine light seems to permeate all human
situations, but, when we return home, we see that opposition
and ill will, envy and jealousy still persist. The "aroma of sanctity"
fades quickly as we're faced with the truth of our human condition.
How is it possible not to become discouraged, not to lose faith?*

⤸

Imagine yourself at a concert. The musicians assemble on the
stage. The discordant sounds of practice runs fill the auditorium.
As the conductor lifts his baton, the audience grows still. Hushed
expectancy gives way to sound. The music soars and speaks of life
— its heights and depths, its shadows and lights. The musicians are
one with their instruments. During the performance, a sense of harmony pervades conductor, players, listeners; they honor the com-
poser, whose music can raise an audience to transcendent heights.

When the concert ends, this harmonious whole breaks into
component parts. "Heavenly artists" become human again! The
pianist relaxes, leans back, and stifles a yawn. The cellist bends over
unceremoniously and picks up a bulgy pocketbook lying beside her
chair. Members of the "enraptured" audience begin leaving before
the conductor has taken his final bows.

Am I Living a Spiritual Life?

I don't want to see the pianist as a middle-aged, balding man; I don't want the cellist to take me back to the world of keys and Kleenex or the anxious crowd to remind me that my car is parked in a bad corner of the lot.

On second thought, why can't I love the sheer humanity of the musicians, who are tired because they've given so much? As I'm carried out with the crowd and back into the current of everyday existence, I try to keep alive the impact of the symphony.

I feel renewed by the force and beauty of these past two hours. The perfection of the music has sharpened my senses. I hear the sounds of voices and traffic; I feel the pulse of ordinary life; I try to appreciate it in a new way because it's the raw material from which music is distilled. I want to hold on to my recharged perceptions, my sense of completeness and harmony.

A retreat, like an evening's concert, is not the whole of life. It's a time of refreshment. It isn't meant to lead me out of this world but to be an entrance into the heart of reality through greater knowledge of self, through opening up to a fuller potential. It's this augmented self that I bring with me to my everyday routine.

If I'm fortunate enough to undergo a stirring experience during a retreat, I can draw upon it as an incentive for further growth. God graces me during this time with a heightened sense of his love and concern. He gives me the kind of spiritual boost I need every so often to help me to live with peace and joy.

If I come home so filled with fervor that I lose sight of the pace and particulars of those around me, I might misuse the bene-fits of my retreat in impulsive attempts to make others change. God gives his light to each of us in his own time. We can do little to hasten the spiritual unfolding of others except by our prayer, ex-ample, and gentle response. If God wills, we can spontaneously open up to these channels of grace.

When we carry our retreat experience with us in the form of greater patience toward those who oppose or exclude us, we hold on to the "aroma of sanctity." We're able to accept more peacefully the tensions and misunderstandings that occur in any community. To live with charity amid opposition and persecution is to do the bidding of our Lord.

When we want to preserve significant moments of family life, we take pictures. Christenings, birthdays, vacations, and like events are fixed on film. Similarly, when we keep a journal during retreat, it serves to recall how we were touched by God; it preserves these valued moments so we can return to them again and again.

The poet Wordsworth stopped to listen to the young reaper singing at her work and noted:

> *The music in my heart I bore,*
> *Long after it was heard no more.*

Looking back on another special moment, he wrote in "I Wandered Lonely as a Cloud":

> *For oft, when on my couch I lie*
> *In vacant or in pensive mood,*
> *They flash upon that inward eye*
> *Which is the bliss of solitude;*
> *And then my heart with pleasure fills,*
> *And dances with the daffodils.*

Wordsworth had no tape of the reaper's song; he didn't pick any of the daffodils, but both experiences remained in his heart, in his "inward eye."

The inner eye perceives what is given; it guides our return to outer action and community concern. As John Donne wrote in his *Devotions Upon Emergent Occasions*:

No man is an island, entire of itself; every man is a piece of the continent, a part of the main. If a clod be washed away by the sea, Europe is the less, as well as if a promontory were, as well as if a manor of thy friend's or of thine own were: any man's death diminishes me because I am involved in mankind, and therefore never send to know for whom the bell tolls; it tolls for thee.

Donne is saying we mustn't separate ourselves from the "flesh and blood" of our life situation. If we step aside momentarily, it's only for the sake of bringing the "continent" of our concern to its deepest source in Christ. Ill will, opposition, envy, and jealousy must be laid at his feet; our efforts alone will not resolve them. These problems live on in all of us because all of us need to be redeemed.

The illusion of retreat can be that I leave the "flesh" of human life behind when I enter into solitude. To correct this deception, it's wise to recall Christ's words to those who wanted to tear out the weeds planted by the enemy. "Let both grow together until the harvest; and at harvest time I will tell the reapers, 'Gather the weeds first and bind them in bundles to be burned, but gather the wheat into my barn' " (Matt. 13:30).

Retreat should be an integrating experience in which I allow my whole life — the wheat and the weeds — to be brought into intimate encounter with the Lord. I bring before him the boss I can't stand, the distressing conflict between me and my neighbor, the explosive anger that hurts unnecessarily. Retreat isn't an escapist trick that removes me from the weeds of enmity and the disintegrating experiences of life. It shouldn't make me believe that utopia is at hand.

A truly Christian retreat puts me in tune with my call to imitate Christ by living his Paschal Mystery. This mystery implies the moment-to-moment passing over from death to new life. If I return from retreat with the expectation of instant perfection, I cease to live in the humble truth that the light of the spirit is always dimmed by the darkness of sin.

Christ himself entered the real world of beauty and ugliness, of trust and betrayal, of humility and pride. He wanted people to bring their struggle with good and evil to him and to seek their salvation from him, not from their own projects of perfection.

Fishermen brought to him their concerns about the catch; tax collectors, the scandal and hatred of their position; Magdalene, her tarnished nature. The leper brought his leprosy; the blind man, his blindness; the cripple, his broken limbs; a mother, her concern for the future of her two sons. Peter brought his lack of courage and his impetuous nature. All came to him to be healed. All felt the dynamics of life and death, light and shadow, harmony and disharmony that mark a fully human life.

To reflect on my life without integrating these tensions is a subtle escape that "diminishes me." When I do so, I'm not accepting that "I'm involved in mankind" — in all of its mystery, redeemed not by our merits but by Christ's love.

In the Gospel account of the Transfiguration, Luke tells us that Jesus took Peter, James, and John to the mountain to pray (cf. Luke 9:28-36). He invited them to retreat with him, away from the crowds, away from their familiar environment. Here they experienced the glory and majesty of Christ in a totally new way. This Jesus, who walked the dusty roads with them, was suddenly transfigured: his face became radiant, his clothes dazzling white.

Caught up in the awesomeness of the experience, Peter wanted to remain there, to continue living in this ecstasy and not to return to the routines of daily life. However, a few moments later,

Am I Living a Spiritual Life?

Jesus stood before them stripped of glory and radiance. Everything around them was as it was before this epiphany.

During retreat, I'm often like Peter. I tell the Lord that it's good to be here, away from community problems and obligations. I have time to pray and reflect, to be more open to the Lord's message for me and his action in my life. Like Peter, I want to cling to this experience of deeper intimacy, to enjoy forever this state of near ecstasy.

By returning to the ordinariness of life "in the valley," Jesus tells us that it isn't possible to remain on the level of heightened religious experience. He invites us to return to our familiar environment, to integrate within our daily situation what has been revealed to us during retreat.

It isn't easy to do so because we tend to isolate our retreat experience from concrete living, where we no longer have as much time to reflect and pray. What was so clear during this time apart slowly begins to disappear. Life becomes more complicated; we're disillusioned when we fail and the euphoria fades.

A reflective turn to the Gospels makes us realize that the disciples too failed many times after witnessing the Transfiguration. They were limited like us. Problems such as duplicity and pettiness persist despite the retreats people make. Strengthened and enriched by the experience of deeper intimacy with Christ, we can become more accepting of these frailties and more merciful toward the human condition.

The real truth of our retreat is the message of the Transfiguration: "Listen to him" (Luke 9:35). By learning to listen to Jesus in the "now" of daily life, we begin to reap the true benefits of retreat. The mountaintop moment can become the background of our daily endeavors in the valley below. The heightened experience isn't lost, for the more we listen to Jesus, the more we're able to integrate what we hear into the art of everyday living.

2

Assessing the Real Situation

*We're open to reality on varying levels, ranging from a
high degree of awareness to near oblivion of the real
situation. How can we learn to listen to reality so that
we can assess the situation properly and prudently?*

Simple situations test the quality of my awareness if I'm alert to
them. Suppose it has been raining for days. I'm tired of the drab
weather. One morning I stop for a moment to watch the bubble
created as a drop of rain falls on a puddle and ripples away. Soon I
notice the esthetic effect of rain falling not only into the puddles
but on everything else. Raindrops form puddles that converge into
rivulets that run to the edge of the street and down the hill into
the river. My thoughts expand to take into account the life-giving
quality of water, its cleansing effects. The rain may remind me of
the unity of all people, for all are in need of its refreshment.

Had I chosen not to be attentive to the rain in this meditative
way, I'd have missed this meaning. My reflective presence to the
life-giving water opens me to insights I had failed to see previously.

When we take time to be present to our situation, we discover
that our perception is deepened; our way of thinking is enlarged.

Am I Living a Spiritual Life?

We learn to watch, to wait, to weigh. We look with a fresh eye. We penetrate beyond the obvious.

How do we see what's really there? How do we have access to reality in its many meanings? The answer is that we usually don't. We're all blinded by our practical projects and prejudices, by our fears, likes, and dislikes. We see, but with our own brand of limited vision.

Reality is all that is; we must accept that our perception encompasses only part of it, according to our limitations. The more conscious we are of them, the clearer our view of reality will be.

For instance, if I know that I'm a dominating type of person, that I tend to take control of situations, this self-knowledge will help me to understand the negative response I get from a colleague who might feel threatened by me. Without this realization I wouldn't have been aware that my particular personality is what evoked her resentment.

Our first task in developing the art of appraisal of the real situation is to know who we are. Everything we observe is filtered through the windows of our self-perception. Often, in the pain and discomfort of focusing on our flaws and faulty vision, we reach an awakening that helps us to see ourselves more realistically and to cope more wisely with our current situation.

Without self-insight, we run the risk of cutting life into predictable shapes and sizes that suit our prejudices. Honest reflection can show us the unexamined influences and assumptions that underpin our view of the world. Every point of closure we recognize makes us more open to reality.

Along with growth in self-awareness, we should attend to awakening from the complacency that threatens to stifle our spirit. If we are content with our narrow view, we might not enjoy the enlightenment God grants. It seems a lot easier to live with tunnel vision, content with life in our safe little cave, than to listen to God's call-ing us into the light.

To add new dimensions to our life requires discipline and the courage to accept the challenges that lie before us. Only in seeing things as they are is it possible to participate in life to the full.

Has a friend ever asked you, "Are you really listening to me?" When you ask him to explain what he means by this question, he might say that he feels as if part of you weren't present. You were listening to snatches of what he was saying. He feels as if you were only vaguely aware of him.

When we don't listen, we might experience a certain emptiness; it evidences our own lack of presence to the situation. Instead of being thrilled with the sounds of life all around us, we echo only an endless monologue of our own thoughts and feelings.

Listening implies abiding in awe-filled attentiveness. I allow the "silent voice" of the situation to appeal to me. This voice can be heard only by one who stops and listens with a minimum of distractions.

Now I enter wholeheartedly into conversation with my friend. Not only do I hear what he has to tell me; I'm also aware of the deeper resonance of love and trust that exist between us, rarely spoken but always present.

Life in the modern world bombards us with such a mass of in-put that we may have to screen ourselves from it until we find a better way to respond to it. All too often, eating, dressing, walk-ing, and other routines lose their spiritual flavor and we start to live them as automatic reflexes.

It can be beneficial for us to break with habitual patterns and allow ourselves to be conscious of the way in which we move from place to place. Certainly a gulped breakfast eaten while reading the paper is less desirable spiritually than gratefully savoring the gift of soft-boiled eggs and buttered toast. The first, fast way often becomes an unnecessary and unfortunate habit.

In the same manner, we group large portions of diffuse information together and label them: Plants or Furniture in one breath and Love or Hatred in another. Some categories are a help in assimilating reality in a peripheral way; others blind us to what's really there. They close us to the rich variety of each particular person, event, and thing. Our superficial grasp of them can lead us to ill-founded conclusions and false assumptions.

Thornton Wilder's play *Our Town* attempts to find the value, above any price, of the smallest event in daily life. Emily, having just died, asks and is allowed to return to a day in her life — her twelfth birthday. As she relives these hours and watches herself going through them, she experiences the anguish of seeing how she and her family, basically loving yet typically human and forgetful, fail to really "look at one another." This sad fact causes Emily to beg to be taken back "up the hill" to her grave before the day is over.

> "But first: Wait!" she cries. "One more look. Good-by, Good-by world . . . Mama and Papa. Good-by to clocks ticking . . . and Mama's sunflowers and food and coffee. And newly ironed dresses and hot baths . . . and sleeping and waking up. Oh, earth, you're too wonderful for anybody to realize you."

Each of us needs in some way to experience a similar return to life. We need to develop a reverent presence to reality, accompanied by a gentle desire to understand the divine directives that come through each situation.

It is the artist who teaches us how to see. We know a painter who leads his students to a field where he asks them to sit about in the grass and take note of some small object — a leaf, an ant, a twig. He tells them to close their eyes and relax completely for a few seconds. Then he asks them to study their chosen object with their whole heart and mind to the exclusion of all else. Notice that he has them first clear their minds in a mode of self-emptying. Only after these steps are they ready to observe their subjects for drawing. Such meditative seeing ought to be imitated by all of us.

We do so much looking but see less and less, so much listening but hear less and less, reading voluminously and appropriating little.

Reality is an expression of the Divine, inexhaustible in its richness. What we receive from it depends on God's grace and the quality of our presence to this unmerited gift. In dying to ourselves — to our fears, desires, needs, prejudices, and defenses, all of which distort reality — we can grasp with St. Paul the power "to comprehend with all the saints what is the breadth and length and height and depth, and to know the love of Christ which surpasses knowledge, that you may be filled with all the fullness of God" (Eph. 3:18-19).

3

Tension of Conflicting Calls

*I feel within myself a peculiar tension, offset, I think, by
two apparently conflicting calls. The Martha in me wants
a busy professional life, the Mary desires contemplation.
How can I reconcile these conflicting sides of myself?*

When was the last time I left my watch at home? Did the hours
not unfold as usual? My "watchless" day was well spent. It also
taught me a valuable lesson about the unnecessary tension caused
by "time-boundedness."

In contrast to this enslavement to scheduling, I might recall
the "timelessness" that goes with a quiet day at the shore. True, it
was necessary to make time for this timelessness, but let's consider
the real question. The problem posed seems less a matter of tension between two apparently opposite calls and more a matter of
realigning our priorities.

Moments of reflection should be woven into my day as a whole.
They should not be "special slots" for which I have to "make time."

Few of us can "get away from it all." What we must try to do instead is "to get more deeply into what is there" — that is, to live
closer to God so that we can sense his presence shining through

every ordinary activity. Obeying his holy will ought to form the ever-present background of my office or teaching schedule, of my balancing accounts or correcting class papers, of my attending conventions or preparing lectures.

The tensions between time and the Eternal usually arise from a split between the "beat the clock" approach toward getting things done and the desire to relax, unwind, and reflect before God. The commitments for which I find myself responsible often can't be altered, but I can change my attitude toward them.

What is this contemplative way I seek? Is it merely a mountain-top experience, or is it the everyday ability to hold on for a moment to what I'm doing, to look at myself in my present situation, and to ponder the mystery that my life is an instrument God uses to build the world into a better place for everyone?

This reflective hold on reality in its Holy Origin isn't limited to set times. It's an attitude of living fully the "now" moment. It can't happen if I'm thinking ahead to what I must do next or "holding off" until I have time for "pure" contemplation. That time might come in a strict monastic setting, but it seldom surrounds the person in the world.

The hands of the clock are always moving in endless circles of seconds, minutes, hours, days, years. They seem to go nowhere, but they travel at great speed. Life moves at an ever-quickening pace the older we grow. The habit of living more reflectively doesn't mean throwing my watch away, being late for everything, or passively flowing with whatever comes along. It's simply a valuable means of adding depth and direction to each moment of my day as I read in it the richness of God's real presence.

The problem of missing this connection is more prevalent than we might think. A friend, burdened with a heavy schedule and the emotional strain of a family crisis, once wrote:

I've thought a lot about the meaning of life this past month — operating as I've had to, under lots of pressure, feeling the pinch of time or lack of it. The quality of life, I discover, depends so much on the small, seemingly insignificant choices we make. I see more and more that who I am is of surpassing value to what I do. I find myself praying not outside of work, as I used to do, but in the midst of things. I bring the whole of my day to the light of the Holy.

This person seems to have found the way to respond to the call to action and to her desire to spend more time in prayer. She responds to this twofold call by pausing, however briefly, and reflecting on her situation in God's light. She couldn't say yes to prayer and no to the professional and familial demands placed on her. She had to reconcile both calls in a deepening awareness of the value of her being. This awareness then renews her doing. She continues:

I've grown in gentleness and respect for myself. Somehow I find this attitude spilling over into my relationships with my family and with others at the office. God has really been with me. I smile at the way I used to act: convinced that a meeting couldn't go on without me; that an office project would never get done unless I did it. What arrogance! Then, following the same style, I would organize time to pray, trying to control God the way I controlled others and myself.

Now I strive to listen in humble openness to myself and my situation. I take into account the demands of body, psyche, and spirit; I try to uncover the unconscious persuaders of ambition, guilt, or fear that blind me to God's call in this situation. When necessary I choose to dive headlong into my work, even increasing time for activity, but in the background I leave room for God to enter my heart. A simple prayer like "Come, Lord Jesus," is always possible, no matter how busy I am. Little wonder I used to live in unbearable tension.

This person has learned to recognize and respond rightly to a twofold call. Now she finds the Martha moments ideal occasions for being creatively faithful to Christ in the Mary-like center of her being.

A misunderstanding of availability can lead to our taking on too much responsibility. It's as if I want to alleviate single-handedly the suffering, ignorance, and despair of the world. In my classroom I feel obliged to implement every new program. I volunteer for extracurricular activities. I petition for safer transportation for preschool children. If there's a cause, I have a solution. At home I try anxiously to resolve family disputes. I'm the first to offer to negotiate neighborhood disagreements, whether others are ready to hear my thoughts or not.

Although I subject my efforts to frequent self-evaluation, I always find more to do — calling my exhaustion the "fruits of Christian charity." I soothe my conscience this way rather than admitting my "savior complex." Secretly, I live with the attitude: "If only I work hard enough, I can eventually solve all the problems of my world, my work, my family."

Caught in this bind, I feel sickened by and increasingly responsible for the lack of love I see all around me. I oblige myself to relieve this condition by tireless work. Any sign of failure or fatigue depresses me. I measure growth by the result of my efforts and the barometer of my successes.

Despite my goodwill, service in this case becomes an obstacle to grace rather than a channel of charity. My work becomes an idol I worship to the exclusion of adoration of the God who loves me not for what I do but for who I am.

Exhaustion might make it impossible for me to exert any more effort. I might have no choice but to stop long enough to listen to God's direction for my life, to appraise the work I must justly fulfill, and to give up those extras triggered by my "savior complex." Only when I accept my gifts and limits can I assess my obligations in God's light.

In prayerful presence to the Incarnate Word, I'm reminded that my role in this world is to be his servant, inspiring others by my relaxed and joyful embodiment of divine directives within the limits of my life situation. The more I evaluate my pursuits in the light of this prayerful call, the less likely I am to take on ministerial roles that might not be his will for me but only a symptom of my own willfulness.

When work interferes with spiritual growth, it becomes empty of its real worth in service of God's reign. The farther I drift away from God, the harder it becomes to incarnate his Spirit in my culture. Instead of pointing to eternal truths that transcend temporal successes, I start to serve the "false gods" of sheer functionalism that emphasize productivity at the expense of a person's dignity. The tension that mounts acts as a catalyst that motivates me either to examine my life or continue to resist God's call.

In science there's a law that states that anything left to itself will tend toward equilibrium. Metal is supposed to possess a certain quality of elasticity. A given amount of stress or tension can be applied to a piece of metal, and, provided it isn't overstressed, it will assume its original shape. The breaking point or the rupture stage is reached when the limit of elasticity is surpassed.

To refrain from stretching a piece of metal beyond the limits of its endurance requires a high degree of moderation. The same applies to achieving a balance between my apostolic endeavors and my need for prayer and contemplative presence.

If I allow career pressures to take precedence over obedience to my calling in Christ, I might come to a breaking point, resulting in an imbalanced, stressful existence. I build my house not on the rock of God's word but on my own agenda.

Prayer must be the mainstay of my professional and apostolic life. The many seemingly wasted moments that arise in an activity-filled day can be times to regain the sense of my primary commitment. These in-between moments act as my bridge to inwardness and the means by which I meet the demands of an active life without losing my equilibrium.

Once my daily presence becomes centered in the Divine Presence, moments of contemplative communion become the sustaining ground of my service. Just as good soil causes a garden to grow and flourish, so contemplation becomes the basis of every worthwhile action.

4

Inner Peace in the Midst of Outer Agitation

Spiritual writers speak of having a "core of inner peace"
in the midst of outer agitation, of recollection in the
midst of work. How can we be at peace inwardly while
outwardly feeling agitated or overloaded with work?

⤳

Picture a pond in winter. A skater pivoting on the ice. A solitary person day after day practicing a figure eight. Turn, reverse, turn — climaxing in a vigorous yet graceful spin. The pivot ends abruptly. The skater glides away to perfect her skill.

What's the secret of such a feat? It's the skater's ability to focus on one object. As long as she concentrates on a tree, a fence, or a point on the distant horizon, she'll maintain her balance.

I too need a point on which to focus if I'm to preserve my equanimity. As the skater's inner calm isn't touched by her whirlwind activity, so too I need a "core of inner peace" enabling me to begin each new action with my feet firmly planted on the ground of contemplation.

The pitch of professional life can reach high speed. The tension of nervous strain begins to affect me. Energy wanes. The direction my life takes is unsteady. There seems to be no stopping.

Am I Living a Spiritual Life?

Now is the time to ask myself whether I've lost my focal point. If so, I need to fix my gaze on Christ, the source of calming union. To maintain a core of inner peace requires that I look deeply enough within to find the indwelling presence of the Prince of Peace. I try to see the circles of activity in which I feel myself dispersed in the light of the Divine Will for me. For the sake of equanimity, I let go of peripheral concerns.

I might discover that the cause of my agitation is a shift from God as center to self as center. To be at peace, I must heed the words of the psalmist: "Trust in him at all times, O people; pour out your heart before him; God is a refuge for us" (Ps. 62:8). These counsels confirm the truth that only the Lord can lay to rest our restlessness in him. Peace is essentially his sheltering gift.

A friend lost her mother after a long and painful illness. She's an outgoing, excitable person, who must have felt the strain of nursing her aged parent, yet she carried on devotedly. After her mother died, she was for others a model of serenity. "What happened to you?" her friends asked. "I learned not to seek for the answer as to why Mother had to suffer so much but to ask only for trust and strength. When the pressures got to be too much and there was nowhere else to turn, I cried out to God in my desperation. The peace I feel is his gift to me. It isn't of my doing."

If I find that my life is generally lived in some degree of agitation, I can't wish away the stress this state causes. Pressures of work and its hurried pace inflict strain upon my physical and emotional being. In the midst of this stress, I ask God to give me peace. I bring the agitations and concerns of my day before the Most High. Looking at them in this light, I pray, "Lord, I have an important meeting with the building supervisor today. Whenever we speak about maintenance matters, I get defensive. Take away this hardness of heart. Help me to realize that he's human too and that all that happens is ultimately in your hands. Whether I succeed or fail, let your will be done."

Such a prayer helps me to realize that the meeting described in this example is a source of inner and outer agitation. Seeing that I might be holding on too tightly to my own ideas prompts me to begin, with God's grace, to let go.

It takes longer on some days than on others to come to restful worship of the Lord. I might need to take a walk in the evening to quiet myself or share my concerns with a friend. These actions help me to recollect myself physically and emotionally. I shouldn't consider them superfluous. I can always find the time to be still or to talk in confidence to someone I trust.

I might notice my pulse beating faster when I now go to that meeting, but I'm better prepared to stay calm. My problems might not be solved as I'd like them to be, but at least agitation lets up and I live in the light of that sacred center where my will is one with God's. There I find peace.

Although Adam and Eve at the start of the Genesis story lived in union with God, free from anxiety and fear, they chose to defy their Creator. As a result they found themselves plunged into sin and shame. Their initial unity was disrupted; their spirit, once free, now found itself bound up in limitations ending in death.

Such is our inheritance: an inner desire for equanimity and peace hampered by a strong tendency to isolate ourselves from God, to become fragmented by our sinfulness, to suffer from our fall from grace.

As spirit self, we reach beyond imagination, reasoning, emotions, and needs toward that which we perceive as infinite. As vital and ego self, we're bound to imagination, reasoning, emotions, and needs, now in conflict due to our finitude. Because of these dynamic forces within us, agitation is inevitable.

There are three ways in which we can handle these disruptions:

• We can let our vital and ego levels "run wild," unleashed and isolated from the influence of our spirit self.

• We can repress them, deny their existence, and keep them under cover while they smolder beneath the surface.

• We can choose to integrate these resistant feelings and functions into the gentle flow of our spirit through faith and the knowledge that we've been redeemed. Under this unifying canopy of meaning, life remains a mosaic of many pieces, but each fits together to form a meaningful whole.

Perhaps a revolving cartwheel might serve as an illustration of this third way. When the wheel is turning slowly, it's obvious that the hub is the axis around which everything rotates. As it gathers speed all the activity seems to move toward the periphery. The further out it goes, the more agitated the action gets. At first glance it seems as if the movements at the fringe are isolated from the rest of the wheel. Meanwhile, the circularity of the hub appears effortless; it becomes almost imperceptible, although it's the dynamic center that keeps the wheel both rotating and grounded.

Faith and my inner core of peace are like the hub of the wheel. They keep me both centered and moving even when my life stumbles into unexpected obstacles along the way to my destiny in God.

I can remember walking home from school one day and suddenly getting caught in a blinding snowstorm. The stinging cold wind and the wet flakes penetrated my skin and sent icy chills up and down my body. As swiftly as possible I sought refuge in the cozy warmth of a neighbor's living room, where a fire crackled in the old stone hearth. What a relief it was to come in out of this turbulence to a haven of peace and security! I was still chilled by the messy weather outdoors, but I had found serenity in the midst of the storm.

There is by way of comparison a calm region in the soul to which we retire for refuge from the outer tumult of life. This zone of stillness in the depths of our being is not a physical place like our living room. It's a spiritual center of peace in Christ in the midst of the agitation of daily life.

What Jesus promised us wasn't a peace without tension; rather he bequeathed to us a peace that would surpass understanding (cf. Phil. 4:7). It would endure regardless of surface disruptions. This peace is best experienced when we keep God's word and obey his will.

Union with God in the core of our being doesn't mean being oblivious to upsetting situations. The difference is that we see them against the horizon of Christ's compassion and the assurance that he will be there with us to meet every challenge.

Such concerns become the means of closer union with the suffering Christ. We might not understand all that God asks of us, yet, in faith and trust, we can say *yes* to the mystery of his will at work in the midst of our concerns. Confidence in Christ gives us the courage to pray:

Lord, along the riverbank, the reeds of the marshland are tossed and ruffled by the wind. How often I've watched storms blow in with their towering force and batter the unprotected reeds flat to the ground in a fury of wind and rain. Yet, when the wind dies down and I stroll by the water's edge, I'm amazed at the triumph of these fragile plants. There they are, upright and erect in the morning breeze. How can a reed bend so low and yet refuse to break? Isn't it because far below the surface of the ground, in the silent depths of its roots, the reed is invulnerable? Even when the wind beats the hardest, the roots sleep on in the depths of the marshland.

I think of myself as a wind-tossed reed. At times I find the world a stormy place. My employers are demanding, my colleagues deceptive, all my best efforts seem to be aborted. I feel miserable in the face of defeat, hurt by a lack of understanding, leveled like the reed by powers that threaten me on all sides. I become harsh with myself and with others. I want to whip my foolishness into shape. All I succeed in doing is to become more and more agitated, filled with self-hate and bitter feelings toward others.

Left to myself in the midst of a storm, I close my eyes and think of you. The disciples were caught just this way on a storm-tossed lake until they awakened you and you calmed the waves. You quieted their fears too, although you reprimanded them for their lack of faith. You tell me that although I'm afraid, if I have faith, I'm not demolished. In the core of my being is your peace.

You have made me a unique person. The contributions I have to make might be limited, but they're my unrepeatable offering of self through you to the world.

A certain peace comes over me. In this moment of inwardness, I recognize anew the value of being who I am. I open my eyes once again to the world around me. I stand erect like a reed, at peace with myself and with you. From this inner peace there flows a new willingness to reach out to others.

I've found more than just myself in this inner core. Below the troubles of my mind and its emotional upsurges, I descend into the spiritual center of my soul. It's difficult to get there, but I allow myself to slip down, to let go . . . knowing that in the sacred cell of self-knowledge I'm held and sustained by an Infinite Peace that surpasses understanding.

Inner Peace in the Midst of Outer Agitation

Here, at a level below all excitation, I'm encompassed by you. In the infinite stillness that surrounds me, dissonance disappears. In the peace of this moment, muscles relax; my mind is free of preoccupying thoughts; the whole of me is enveloped in the sustaining power of your peace.

When I return to work, Lord, let me be a witness to this miracle of inner equanimity in the midst of outer agitation. Let me mirror in some way the mystery of your love, the power of your peace.

5

Involvement with Social Issues

How can we reconcile our longing for
the spiritual life with the pressure to
become more involved in social issues?

An old gardener is planting rose bushes. Intent on his work, he hoes the earth, adds fertilizer, pulls out weeds. While watching him, we become aware of a rhythm in his work. Every so often he steps back and surveys what he has done. How effective was the arrangement of new bushes in the garden? How well were they positioned in relation to the rising and setting of the sun?

What strikes us as unforgettable is his complete involvement in both dimensions of his work — the manual labor itself and the contemplative gaze upon its results. To him both acts are equally necessary to achieve the beautiful results he has in mind.

An oft-quoted passage from *The Little Prince*, by Antoine de Saint-Exupéry, comes to mind here: "It is the time you have wasted for your rose that makes your rose so important." The word *wasted* implies time spent in a non-utilitarian way. As the fox in *The Little Prince* says, "It is only with the heart that one can see rightly; what is essential is invisible to the eye."

Am I Living a Spiritual Life?

In my concern to be more involved in social issues, I can ask myself whether I've lost sight of the basic truth that I'm a finite being who depends on God for everything.

Is the fatigue I feel a result of honest work, or is it a sign of needless worry?

The more demanding a task is, the more necessary it is to survey it from a distance. This objective stance increases my understanding of what I do and why. Such a contemplative perspective helps me to see what God wants of me. It prevents me from buying into the slogan "I can do anything if I put my mind to it."

God calls most of us to be ordinary laborers in the vineyard. He asks us to put his holy will before any thought of erratic heroism or self-inflicted sacrifices. Our main motive must be to move through each day in touch with the mystery. More often than not we're presented with an opportunity to listen with patience to someone in search of support. We needn't wait for an extraordinary moment to do God's will.

In the initial stages of involvement, we're usually so preoccupied with what has to be done that we have little time left to pray and reflect on our lives. They're too full. As the routine of work sets in and we adjust to its demands, we begin to take a closer look at ourselves and at the issues for which we feel responsible.

A vague feeling of emptiness inside — despite the flurry of activity outside — leads us to reclaim our longing for a deeper spiritual life that alone can sustain us. Christ has to be our center. It is in, with, and through him that we minister to others. Our presence to Jesus permeates our participation in the working world. We don't abandon our service to society; we bring to it the depth of charity that flows from our life with the Lord.

Instant integration isn't possible. It takes time to balance activity and recollection. This rhythm weaves its way through every fiber of our life. Priorities are reordered, blind spots removed, values restored — all with the help of grace. Inspiration and incarnation become part of our everyday routine. The world of spirit is wed to the world of social service.

Always the balance has to be there. Only if I bring Christ with me can I find him in the marketplace. In other words, the effectiveness of my social involvement corresponds to the depth of my spiritual life. I can't give to others what I don't try to live myself.

My daily union with the Lord awakens the realization of my complete dependence on him. I can succeed in what I do only to the degree that I realize that it's God's will I seek, not merely tangible results or immediate rewards.

Candles come in various shapes and sizes. Whether they're used for decoration or for light in an emergency, all of them possess a common element: the wick. Small and insignificant as it might be, the wick makes the candle what it is. Without it, a candle remains a useless piece of wax.

Like the candle, I too need the wick of a deeper spiritual life. Without this dimension, my involvement risks degenerating into mere activism. How can I nourish my prayer life and keep this wick from burning out in the midst of so many commitments? I find the answer when I look to the Lord.

Christ chose a life of selfless service, but he knew when to pause in presence to the Father in prayer. He would at times disappear from the crowd and go off by himself to a deserted place (cf. Mark 6:31). To be faithful to the will of the Father, he had to make time in his life for meditative reflection.

Jesus tells me by his example that I need periodically to slow down my hectic pace, to enter into the depths of my being, and to get in touch with my truest self — with Christ in me. During these moments of prayerful reflection, I try to discern the Father's will in dialogue with my personal and communal calling.

The apparent opposition between spiritual life and worldly involvement fades. My primary concern becomes listening to what God asks of me. Sooner than later this inspirational insight permeates my social actions.

Just as a candle is of little value without a wick, so my most sincere commitments risk losing their witness value without a deepening of the contemplative dimension.

6

Prayer and the Problem of Fatigue

*How often we hear people say — even after a good
night's sleep — "I'm tired." Would you comment on fatigue
in general and particularly its bearing on the life of prayer?*

It goes without saying that we can't pray and sleep at the same
time. If I rise in the morning, stumble around in a semiconscious
state, and then try to pray, it's no wonder I can't stay awake.

Fatigue dulls our attention and our powers of concentration; it
causes us to be irritable; it weakens our sense of resoluteness.
Trying to meditate at such times results only in frustration.

"Suffering from morning fatigue" might be another way of saying "not fully awake." Still, morning might be the only time I have
for meditation. I rise hurriedly, dress quickly, swallow breakfast,
stop at a church on the way to work, kneel or sit, begin to pray,
then promptly drift off to sleep.

Such prayer is hardly comparable to what Thomas Merton de-
scribes as an inner awareness of God's direct presence or an awakening of our inner self. This awakening requires that my physical
body be sufficiently stimulated to listen to the stirrings of God in
my deepest self. Fatigue arises for various reasons. The first and

most obvious is that I might not be getting enough rest to restore my body after its normal activity. Many of us take on more than we can manage. Regardless of our altruistic motives, if we continue to augment an already crowded schedule, we're bound to lose our effectiveness and perhaps our health as well.

Certainly when we ignore the signals from our physical self that point toward tension and excessive fatigue, we're at risk of disregarding God's will speaking in our vital limits. Eating properly and getting adequate fresh air, sleep, and exercise are basics for a sound spiritual life.

Fatigue can result from psychological causes. There are monotonous winter days when I wonder how I'll stay awake after the last class to finish an assignment, to say nothing of going to chapel for prayer. I feel dejected and listless. A glass of milk and a nap seem more in order than trying to study or pray. I decide to go home. As I open the lock, I find some letters the postman has slipped under the door. "At least I got some mail," I think — and not only "some" mail but a special letter from a dear friend and an invitation to come and visit her in two weeks. Instant cure. No headache, no fatigue, no blues. I'm alive with enthusiasm that carries over to the study and prayer I had intended to postpone.

My initial weariness wasn't imaginary. The fact was that my ordinary routine had fallen into a state of sheer drudgery. Fatigue took root in spiritual listlessness, in a lack of meaning. Boredom and a general feeling of malaise had crept into my life.

Many of us experience a similar sluggishness. We are especially vulnerable to the noise and clatter of modern life and the feeling of being overwhelmed by so much input. We're less adept at handling resentments and pettiness. We become tense with the pressures of competition; we're disappointed by our lack of achievement and crushed by the materialistic thrust that urges us to have what's beyond our reach. At other times, we move through life disgruntled with the people around us and the places in which we have to work.

All of these forces, and many others like them, cause me to experience some degree of anger and resentment. I wait for a friend; she's late and I explode. Someone rejects me; I respond defensively. One of the major manifestations of either expressed or repressed anger is depression. There are few of us who don't suffer from it in some measure along with the anger and self-pity that accompany it.

Nothing brings on fatigue faster than these three ills. Even during the most frenetic period of compulsive overwork we can find ways to get recharged. By contrast, depression empties us of vitality. It's a state of withdrawal, a form of giving up. If we can't pull out, we might slip into despair. Sleep is a welcome reprieve, but as long as we remain depressed, not even a good night's rest can replenish us.

Whether we suffer major depressions due perhaps to overwhelming and unresolved problems or mild bouts due to the ordinary pressures and disappointments of daily life, we experience some sense of isolation. The awareness of God recedes into the background; we feel tired and alone, filled with so many problems that it's hard to pray.

It might be necessary to seek professional help through counseling and spiritual direction to lift the cloud of fatigue that engulfs us when we feel lonely, angry, and depressed. Rest is essential in healing both physical and psychological fatigue. From a spiritual perspective, so is quiet listening to God. In this context, fatigue can be seen as a call to examine my life and affirm once again the primary goal I seek: love of God and neighbor.

One way of coping with fatigue is to take note of how tense I am. A wrinkled forehead, a clenched jaw, a rigid neck are the symptoms that remind me that dealing with excessive stress is never easy, but it needs to be done. I might begin by consciously relaxing and letting go. I surrender to God all the tiredness I feel. I sense a lessening of my fears, a letting go of my unresolved problems and the unconscious pressures I place upon myself. Gratitude to God replaces self-pity; peace lessens anger. The last remnants of doubt disappear since I'm sure that God has heard my cry and with loving solicitude relieved the tension and fatigue that drained my spirit. In childlike trust, I stop trying to solve my own problems and allow him to give rest to my soul (cf. Matt. 11:28-30).

7

Recovering Religious Attitudes

*Is there any way to recover the religious attitudes of joy,
wonder, and gratitude that seemed more prevalent in the past?
Is it possible for a self-centered, uncharitable, and demanding
person to change enough to mirror consonance with the Lord?*

Just as good ground is necessary to liberate the blossom from the
seed, so is a receptive heart necessary to release the religious attitudes of joy, wonder, and gratitude hidden in every soul. These virtues are meant to mature and bear fruit, yet they often seem absent
from our lives. Perhaps it's because we live in a period that places
so much emphasis on productivity that we've lost sight of the inner attitudes from which all apostolic activity must blossom forth.

Like seeds sown among thorns, these virtues might have been
choked off by our anxiety over the demands of an active life cut off
from contemplative presence to the Lord. Preoccupation with
professional competence might have led us to overdevelop our
ambitious, aggressive decisions at the expense of our more receptive dispositions.

Our tendency to totalize professionalism can push joy, wonder, and gratitude to the sidelines of our life. Competence ceases

to be at the service of Christ and becomes instead an unhappy, self-centered end in itself.

In Dostoevsky's novel *The Brothers Karamazov*, a character named Zossima, an elder of the monastery near the village, was prized by the people for his wisdom and sought by many for counsel. Zossima was drawn most to the sinful among those who visited him; it seemed to the monk that the greater the sinner, the more love he had for him, since these troubled people best represented the souls Christ had come to save.

The moment self-centered, demanding persons recognize their faults and admit their need for redemption, they become signs of hope. The Lord looks at their efforts, not at their failures. He loves them in their weakness.

Such spiritual transformation is a lifelong process. It can't be hastened according to my timetable. If I change, it will be God's doing, not mine. Self-condemnation does nothing to lighten the load of guilt I already carry. Needed is compassion for my own and others' vulnerability. Perhaps the only way I'll be freed to experience the virtues of joy, wonder, and gratitude is by seeing in myself and in others a reflection of the merciful forgiveness of my Savior.

In the letter to the Hebrews, we read about the compassionate high priest who ". . . can deal gently with the ignorant and wayward, since he himself is beset with weakness" (Heb. 5:2).

Zossima, the holy man, knew what it was to be gentle and nonjudgmental. God alone knows the turmoil tearing apart a person's heart. We can be compassionate when we see signs of weakness in others because we know we share them. Perhaps the person I label as uncharitable labels me as judgmental. Both of us need to be redeemed.

Especially sad is the case of a person who refuses to grow to spiritual maturity, who doesn't radiate the joy, wonder, and gratitude that seem to be the spontaneous outgrowth of a life of intimacy with the Trinity.

Many reasons could be given for this condition, but one seems especially pertinent. The transcendent dimension of this person's self no longer permeates the other levels of his or her personality. At some point the person has allowed functionalism to become the motivating factor in his or her life — following social rules of conduct and a strict work ethic without attunement to the meaning that comes from being enlightened by the Spirit.

Life has become a robotic reaction rather than a Spirit-centered response. The person can no longer find the inner resources he or she needs to imbibe the spiritual nourishment a humane community has to offer.

When our life lacks meaning, is there anything that can be done to restore us to a vibrant path of joyful spirituality?

When we find ourselves dying for lack of inner nourishment, we might need to return to the wellspring of all spirituality, the Holy Spirit, the source of our religious attitudes. No one formula for restoration covers every case of depletion because God's ways aren't our own.

It's easy to presume that all Christians should be happy until we witness the amount of unhappiness in our own lives. If we humbly accept this fact, we might be able to hear Christ's call to convert our hearts. Unloving limitations will always be within us and others due to sin, but, with Christ's help, we can reach our fullest potential as spiritual persons.

Without this disposition of surrender, we might continue to count on our own strength when all we ought to count on is the support of the Lord. We might begin to rebuild our lives on the basis of our own self-image rather than on the glory and praise of God.

Am I Living a Spiritual Life?

As a fallen race, we might never know what demons of heredity or history cling obsessively to our own and others' heart, impeding the way to joy, wonder, and gratitude. We can't always discern to what extent our inner vision has been distorted by past experiences or how seriously our unconscious system of defenses works against the call to be faithful to the Christ-form of our soul.

Compassion clears our vision and allows us to see the crosses others carry. We pray that suffering will be for them a purifying experience and that they will respond generously to the call of grace God has allowed to echo in their lives. In spite of repeated failures, they've tried to overcome their faults. It could be that their life reflects a series of sinful rejections of God's mercy, but it isn't our place to judge anyone ultimately.

Christ asks, "How can you say to your brother, 'Let me take the speck out of your eye,' when there is the log in your own eye?" (Matt. 7:4). What we can confirm is that salvation is from the Lord; it doesn't come from our efforts or spiritual exercises. Our only hope lies in the mercy of God. Transformation is his gift; it doesn't depend on our track record of religious achievements.

The blessing given to the most spiritual person in the world would become a curse the moment he or she rested in satisfied complacency, as if life were a series of investments entitling one to find favor with God. When another's condition, be it self-centered and uncharitable, reminds us of our common sinfulness, then perhaps he or she has fulfilled the special mission of reminding all members of the Christian community of our need for redemption. Only then may we recover the religious attitudes of joy, wonder, and gratitude that signify our total reliance on the Lord.

Part 3

Living Christian Community

1

Building Human Relations on Trust

*I realize that all human relationships must be built on trust.
What do we do when we learn from experience that a person
can't be trusted — when, for example, he or she reveals
a confidence that hurts the reputation of another person?*

When we're not able to trust another person because of past experiences, innate common sense seems to dictate that in some way we must monitor our interactions with that person.

Despite a proven inability to trust a person with confidences, we may still trust in his or her underlying goodwill. Our response to the person can vary depending on the circumstances we share. A pervasive resentment can affect our relationship from the point of distrust to the present moment. Once the immediacy of the incident passes, we must move beyond these negative responses and seek to follow the words of the apostle Paul: "[Love] . . . does not rejoice at wrong, but rejoices in the right. Love bears all things, believes all things, hopes all things, endures all things" (1 Cor. 13:6-7).

We might question the goodwill of others, but we needn't extend this distrust to their whole person. Perhaps in this specific incident they betrayed confidentiality and now deserve another chance. We only diminish ourselves if we take pleasure in the weakness of spirit another displays.

Life teaches us that we must remain as open to the human potential for sin and failure as for grace and redemption.

What if I'm the one who has lost the trust of others and am now seeking to regain it? Trust isn't something I can demand. It's a relationship I earn by the way I live. Whether I'm the giver or the receiver of trust, I need to believe in the potency for goodness, honesty, and sincerity in each person I meet.

Without this belief in the basic goodness of others, I leave them no room for change or growth. I simply put them in a slot labeled "never to be trusted."

Am I able to take the risk and believe in someone who has on several occasions shown himself or herself to be untrustworthy? I can do so only if I believe that every human being has the potential to change. He or she is a mystery, known only to God. No one can predict in advance how grace might move another's heart.

Even though a person has shown himself or herself as lacking in the virtue of trust once, twice, or several times, it doesn't mean that the person will remain that way forever. Surely the words of Jesus to Peter, when he wanted to know how many times to forgive his brothers, are applicable here: "I do not say to you seven times, but seventy times seven" (Matt. 18:22).

St. Paul wrote to the Galatians about a test of trust we ought to take into account: "But when Cephas came to Antioch I opposed him to his face, because he stood condemned. For before certain men came from James, he ate with the Gentiles; but when they came he drew back and separated himself, fearing the circumcision party" (Gal. 2:11-12). Peter, in this instance was, according to Paul, not behaving in a trustworthy manner. Paul confronted this Rock who had been commissioned personally by Jesus to feed his lambs: "But when I saw that they were not straightforward about the truth of the gospel, I said to Cephas before them all, 'If you, though a Jew, live like a Gentile and not like a Jew, how can you compel the Gentiles to live like Jews?' " (Gal. 2:14). This reprimand was undoubtedly unpleasant, but Peter's humble openness, combined with Paul's courage, came together for the good of the Christian community.

This passage shows how vulnerable Peter was despite the position he held, how easily he was swayed by the presence of the "circumcision party." His dealings with the community in this situation were wavering and weak. Paul's action, painful though it must have been, sprang from his fundamental trust in Peter's goodwill. What he didn't trust was the validity of Peter's action or the wisdom of his motivation. Seeing through this mistake, he put his trust on a deeper plane. He trusted that Peter, limited though he was in this regard, could still be open to the truth, admit his mistake, and change accordingly. He trusted the veracity of his own conscience and the fact that he was obliged to act upon it.

This is the kind of trust needed in any community. We're all fallible and weak. At times our actions are unwise and our motivations aren't pure. We need others to convince us that we can be open to the truth and that we're able to change and grow once we see it. It takes courage to operate with this kind of trust. It can mean facing a superior with what appears to be a case of showing unfair favoritism to others or speaking to a friend about divulging privileged information. It doesn't mean we suddenly have to become the conscience of the community, judging others while exonerating ourselves.

Building trust in community begins with me. It means being open to the suggestions and criticisms of others, to the importance of praying and deliberating before I decide what to do, to bearing responsibility for my own insights, especially when they prove to be wrong. The openness I feel in myself sets the tone for trust in the community.

If I find that a person I trusted — for instance, someone in authority — has revealed what I assumed to be confidential information, my first response is naturally to feel angry and hurt by this betrayal: "A person who holds a position of authority should respect the private communications of others and keep them confidential!"

Time passes and I'm able to look at the situation more objectively. Is there anything I can do to build a more trusting atmosphere? Should I confront this person in a kind way and express how I really feel? Could it be that he or she isn't aware of having revealed my confidence?

I can't undo what has been done, nor can I, for several reasons, decide never to speak to this person again. Because of his or her position of authority, the person will continue to play an important role in my life. This fact might lead me to further reflection on my own inner attitudes.

God allowed this event to happen. Although I find it hard to understand why, I still want to accept that God has chosen to test my trust in this way. Although I've been a victim of human weakness, the betrayal has taught me the value of confidentiality for those in authority.

If and when I confront the person who spoke out of turn, another side of the story might emerge. I might find that, from the person's perspective, what happened was construed not as a betrayal of trust but as a sharing of truth. The person acted without realizing how I'd feel, but in what he or she believed would be in the best interest of all.

Now I question whether I'm making unrealistic demands for perfection. Can I allow for occasional mistakes on the part of those in leadership positions? Naturally, if trust is betrayed habitually, I must be cautious. How I respond depends on the nature, severity, and frequency of the offenses.

Even if I need to be cautious before divulging similar confidences to others, I can still trust in their overall goodwill and potential for growth in the context of trustworthy exchanges.

"Moreover it is required of stewards that they be found trustworthy," says St. Paul (1 Cor. 4:2). If this requirement is lacking altogether, certainly I should do what I can to have the person in leadership replaced by one who is more qualified, but without resorting to tactics that are untruthful, dishonest, or unjust.

2

Conflict in Community

The ideal of living our Christian commitment in community is often marred by either "submerged" or "open" conflict. Is there a way of handling these attitudes so that they don't destroy community but lead ultimately to its strength and growth?

If we want to understand the problem of conflict in community, we have to start by accepting its reality in our own lives. Think of the ambivalence we feel when we have to choose between two equally attractive alternatives.

Friends encourage me to vacation with them at their summer place; at the same time I receive a month-long summer research grant. I feel torn between my need to relax after a trying school year and my desire to advance in my chosen field.

This ordinary human experience reminds us that ambivalence emerges in the midst of interaction with the people and events that make up our daily world. To be alive is to be in conflict. It is to be faced with the challenge of choice. An array of attractions opens up before me, and I realize that I can never actualize all of them. Conflict reminds me of my human limitations. In saying yes to one possibility, I must say no to others.

Am I Living a Spiritual Life?

Since community is a collection of unique individuals, it follows that personal conflicts will never cease. More likely than not, they'll be intensified. My idea of what makes for a successful group experience often clashes with the vision held by others. We might share a common goal, but chances are we approach it in different ways.

Conflict arises when we both insist that our way is the best one to implement the common good. Tempers flare. Misunderstandings arise, and we feel discouraged.

The answer isn't to pout in anger but to see what's happening as an opportunity for personal and communal growth. The deepest maturation happens not when we resolve our differences, but when we remember that our life in community depends on God's grace and on the constant cooperation of all of us who live and work together.

While we're each endowed with unique gifts to share, we must be willing to defer to the common good. Conflict isn't a signal to pack up and leave the scene but to become a reconciling presence, to remain in touch with our true potential while finding ways to foster peace with others.

How well we handle situations of conflict can be the test of our spiritual growth. For example, as a teacher, I advocate individualized instruction rather than trying to direct a whole class. Another teacher opposes this approach. Having conducted a well-disciplined seventh grade for years, she's convinced that only in a structured situation can a teacher command respect. In my mind she always seems to be making little speeches for my benefit and mocking my teaching methods. I feel threatened, but I push these negative emotions to the background while becoming increasingly upset. I try to avoid her as much as possible.

What can I do to handle this conflict? I could express my anger immediately, either by an explosive blow-up or by letting it seep through in the icy tones of my response. Neither of these solutions, however, would change her attitude. Even if I admit my angry feelings, patterns of politeness must be observed. The "silent treatment" is no solution either.

A more responsible answer might be to let go of my preoccupation with a new teaching method and wait until the opposition is less intense, less governed by feelings, and more open to reason. I might fume in the privacy of my room, but later I'll probably have to admit that there are also merits to the other teacher's method.

Perhaps compromise is possible to keep the peace in our small teaching community. Why let an overbearing or touchy attitude on either side threaten our commitment to the students? Perhaps in the future the topic can be discussed in a more open, less defensive way. For now we can cope with conflict without denying the possible truth of both positions. It's better to preserve the norms of courtesy and respect for the uniqueness of the other than merely to win a point.

It's impossible and even unhealthy to try to root out all conflict from community. Conflict is necessary for growth. A plant pushing through the hard-packed earth struggles against its environment to get the nourishment it needs. A child in conflict with his or her parents learns more about who he or she is. Elements of conflict are also essential to our spiritual self-formation in that they spark reflection and personal decision-making.

Conflict is like a tension that results in action or reaction. Consider a slingshot. Too much tension breaks the elastic; too little makes it inefficient. This delicate balance isn't easy to maintain. When conflict increases beyond the breaking point, I might try to repress it, but smoldering resentment can become hazardous.

Burying feelings without any kind of insight or resolution only postpones or intensifies the issue. Submerging conflict isn't the answer, but how and when do I bring it out into the open? *How* depends on my own sensitivity, on past experience, and on the graces I receive. *When* depends on my judgment — which should be enlightened by the Holy Spirit — of the most appropriate opportunity to express what I'm feeling.

Again we see the need for insight. If I'm completely honest with myself, I might detect my own compulsive or resentful behavior. Then I can be more objective about the attitudes of others. I can reach beyond the immediacy of a situation to the goodwill inherent in every person. Prayerful recollection is always needed to deepen my receptivity to the light of the Holy Spirit.

Experience will tell me when our relationship is too brittle for confrontation or when the time is right for a frank discussion and a defusing of the tension.

To bring differences into the open involves risk. I might inadvertently hurt the other person by openly expressing my point of view. Although my intention is to do good, my action might result in pain. I might start out calmly enough but find my anger getting the best of me. Old accumulated hurts might flare up. I'm shocked to find what a "slush fund" of animosity is bottled up inside of me. I end up losing control when all I wanted to do was to find a way to disagree agreeably!

Expressions of conflict can have positive results only if they flow from a deep source of love and concern for others. Subtle traces of pettiness or hostility signal a failed relationship, whereas conflict that springs from honest disagreement can be an instrument of growth. If each member of the community longs for the transcendent good of the whole, conflict won't be reduced to backbiting or squabbling.

Knowing my own weakness before God generates gentleness and patience. This loving concern comes not from me but from

Christ living in me. He said that he came to bring not only peace but the sword (cf. Matt. 10:34-36). Did he mean that conflict must necessarily result when we seek to do the Father's will? Or is he showing us that conflict can be a blessed occasion for growth in candor, courage, and compassion?

3

Destruction of Community by Negativity

*Is it possible that the prevalence of a spirit of
negativity could destroy a community? How
can we best guard against negative attitudes?*

The uncharitable, the troublesome, the dissenters. We decry
them and shake our heads in indignation. "What will happen to
our community with them around?" we ask.

I see these naysayers and sigh at the thought of having to live
and work with them. "My life can't be effective in such an atmosphere," I think. "How can those who are uncharitable and disrup-
tive of community be living a spiritual life? Do they draw their
strength from diminishing one another? What is it that drives
them on and elicits negativity?"

Each of us has defects, but these weaknesses are not what destroy a community. What does cause its demise is the failure of
each member to respect his or her unique-communal calling and
to live in union with Christ. The actual force of our presence to
God counteracts the subtle traces of negativity, which the Evil
Spirit uses to counteract the work of the Holy Spirit in a loving
community.

Am I Living a Spiritual Life?

When a spirit of negativity prevails among us, our first impulse might be to blame rigid structures or to assume that merely worldly dispositions are destroying our religious spirit. The truth is that some kind of negative spirit might reside in the heart of each member of a community.

Think of the petty strife that escalates when one group is closed off from another. Hurt feelings smart; cruel words are exchanged. If each member of a faction were searching sincerely for the will of God, differences of opinion could be powerful agents of promoting new life instead of contributing to mutual destruction.

Complaining and gossiping are highly infectious. They are a means of getting attention and of controlling others. Listening to gossipy details is part of the virus of grumbling. Often we are eager to collect these tidbits that mar another's reputation and, of course, the most newsworthy are always negative.

When people feel a lack of excitement or challenge in their lives, they latch on to these negating currents and augment them to enhance their own sense of importance. It takes a conscious effort not to encourage what appear to be harmless remarks by neither listening to them nor spreading them further.

When the light of the Holy Spirit invades my hardened heart, it prompts me to forgive others' hurtful deeds and cutting words. I don't double the problem by responding to negativity in kind. I try instead to take a positive approach: to see and do what is good; to operate less on the surface level of negativity and more from motives of forgiveness, trust, and mutual confirmation.

It's the underlying presence of the Holy Spirit that motivates our spirit of togetherness. This sustaining spirit is present especially in my responses to the people I meet day in and day out. Desire for intimacy with God encourages me to be more open to them so that the warmth of the Spirit becomes my own.

Destruction of Community by Negativity

The Holy Spirit protects me when other "spirits" threaten to prevail within the community. I'm able to deal with a noisy, non-recollected atmosphere, an obsessive work orientation, negligence in worship, or my own uncharitableness if I allow the Holy Spirit to temper my negative reactions with the grace of a truly Christian response.

Picture living in a situation where a person is greatly misunderstood and ill treated because she hasn't conformed to the "expected" behavior set by the group. Her approach to a task conflicts with "standard procedures," and consequently she's labeled a "troublemaker." She's criticized for being different, for not following the rules, for giving in to personal whims. Lack of understanding could make her bitter, but she's mature enough to see beyond such gossip. She doesn't go to pieces because of it. She believes that she's doing good work. As time goes by and she fails to fulfill the gossiper's predictions, people are able to accept her and even to give her encouragement and support. Rather than dragging herself down to the level of negative ridicule, she edifies others by her kindly response.

The "wrong spirit" is always deceptive and divisive. It thrives on gossip and gripes but soon dissolves under the impact of virtuous living. This change of heart doesn't mean that every member of the community will become a model Christian; it does mean that each person must try, within her limits and shortcomings, to aim for the limitless goodness of living like Christ. He alone can turn the darkness to light and redeem us from the sins that divide our community.

Even the chronic complainer is a person pleading for understanding and love. His or her usual response is to continue to cause heartache, but beneath this bleak exterior is a person longing for the light of Christ. He's the loving source who gives a person seeking to be good the strength to prevail over evil.

Am I Living a Spiritual Life?

The spirit of Christian community is charitable because it's built on each person's obedient response to the inspiration of the Holy Spirit in service of the common good. If I find myself becoming uncharitable, I know I'm harboring a negative spirit. I need to turn as quickly as possible to the deeper Spirit within me, to Christ, who is the center of my life. Instead of reacting negatively to differences of opinion, I try to turn my attention to how much people are suffering in my community and to empathize with what they're going through.

The Holy Spirit teaches us the art of living compassionately. When we sink into the pit of pettiness, gossip, willfulness, and impatience, we forfeit the call to be another Christ. We allow the negative spirit, the spirit of evil, to gain ascendance. This divisive spirit diminishes both the persons who harbor it and the ones upon whom they vent its venom. Such negativity can cause the destruction of an entire community.

Although weakness and sin will always be mingled with our graced efforts to live Christ's suffering and love, it's only this compassion that can carry us forward. Only if we remain alive in God will we be able to withstand the daily dyings that purify our hearts and promote lasting growth in community.

4

True Values in Community Life

*How can the higher values of the spirit be lived in a community
where non-essentials take precedence over personal creativity
and spiritual deepening? How can we best deal with an
emphasis on external appearances, cleanliness, and rigidity
of schedules to the neglect of personal-spiritual growth?*

The lot of the prophet is to be the one who sees beyond what
others behold. We too need to ascertain whether our vision of the
situation is the correct one. A biblical example might facilitate
our appraisal.

When the Israelites complained about Moses' prolonged stay
on Mount Sinai, it was because they were deprived not only of the
comfort of his presence but also of Yahweh's, which was tangible
for them through him. They built their golden calf much less out
of wickedness than out of their strong desire to have a God they
could see with their human eyes (cf. Exod. 32:1-6).

We all build golden calves that we're inclined to equate with
God. We worship a clean house, rigid schedules, order, and prompt-
ness. These are good practices, especially because we can see and
control them. They gleam like gold in the here and now.

Am I Living a Spiritual Life?

Cleaning house might be valued more highly than speaking to someone in need because it's a tidy, immediately rewarding project. Speaking to another has no neat boundaries, no built-in rewards. I can say to God, "I've done your will because I've cleaned this room perfectly," but who of us can say, "I've done your will because I've loved this person perfectly?"

Because we're all makers of golden calves, we need to show mercy to one another. It was Moses' task to seize the golden calf, burn it, grind it into powder, and scatter the powder on the Israelites' drinking water (cf. Exod. 32:19-20). It's unlikely that we'll be called to act with such rigor, but neither should we ignore this warning. We mustn't worship any idol in place of God. We have to appraise every situation from a scriptural point of view, softened by compassion and the assurance of God's forgiveness. When the occasion arises, we might find ways to make community living more just, merciful, and respectful. Then the way we clean house or come on time to community prayer can be seen as an opening, however small, to spiritual deepening.

If I'm striving to grow in virtue, I can trust that other members of my community are doing the same. We have to give one another the benefit of the doubt. Perhaps I have a special gift for getting to the heart of the matter rather than being caught up in non-essentials. Not everyone has the same sensitivity, which is why my intention to contribute to the common good can evoke misunderstanding. God still may choose me to be as a source of inspiration to others who are striving to live the deeper values cherished by all.

The ideal of community living is to support the worth and dignity of every person. This aim can be a challenge to embody, but to forfeit it can result in an erosion of the common good and can lead individuals to go along with the group to avoid feeling alone.

Looked at from this angle, it might be that the values of those with whom I live and work aren't so different from my own. Because everyone practices virtue in his or her unique way, what might at first glance seem incompatible with my own approach might simply be another way of striving to imitate Christ. Others might at times misjudge my sensitivity to their needs and accuse me of prying into their business. My way of praying might appear to them as overly pious when all I'm doing is trying my best to follow the movements of the Spirit.

What sustains me under this kind of criticism are my honest efforts to follow the Lord's call. As I discover day by day what he asks of me and try my best to fulfill this commission, I find that I'm growing in my relationship with him. At the same time, I strive to grow in sensitivity to the feelings of others by not upsetting them unnecessarily by word or deed.

We can't deliberately change the habits of those around us, but we can have an influence on them by our quiet fidelity to the common good. Our life itself can become a silent witness to Christ in a way no words could. We neither try to impose our convictions on others nor insist that they, not we, have to change. Our loving presence is the best communicator of spiritual values.

Living community life implies respect for the gifts God gives to each member of the Body of Christ. One person's weakness can be compensated for by another's strength. The person who is obsessed with cleaning probably keeps the house in good order while the one addicted to scheduling sees to it that meetings begin and end on time.

If we begin to think that exterior observance is the essence of community life, we might take on the attitude of the Pharisee who did all that was proper but with an empty heart. He stood before the Lord, grateful that he wasn't like the rest of men. Jesus denounced his prideful ways and praised the publican (cf. Luke 18:9-14). This man also fasted, contributed to the temple, and prayed, but he came before the Lord as a sinner humbly begging for mercy. Jesus teaches us that it isn't what we say with our lips that counts but the attitude of heart with which we honor him.

To do good deeds and then pat ourselves on the back because we've done them is hardly an exercise in humility. To enter into these deeper levels of living, we must be motivated by love.

The higher values of the spirit don't exist in a vacuum; they incarnate themselves in the ordinary ways in which we live in the world with others. These common ways are the conduits through which we show our love and respect for community.

To pour coffee in the morning, to be on time for a meal, to clean the garage, to answer the telephone, to take someone to the doctor — all of these acts can be labeled "trivia" we have to get out of the way to get on to the "higher things of the spirit," or they can be transformed by loving hearts and hands. It's easy to get caught in the idea that spiritual values must be expressed in heroic ways, whereas what is the truly heroic is usually hidden in everyday routines.

St. Paul wrote in his letter to the Romans, "I do not understand my own actions. For I do not do what I want, but I do the very thing I hate" (Rom. 7:15). When we find ourselves caught up in busy work to the exclusion of being kind to others, we know what St. Paul means. Although we don't really intend to become so tied up with tasks that we're not available to people, that happens despite our best intentions.

We all know those times when we'd rather not talk to someone because we're too busy. Perhaps the problem is that we spend too much time concentrating on schedules. Unlike people, schedules are predictable. We fear the loss of security that comes when we venture into uncertain situations. Attempting to comfort others is much riskier than polishing a floor. There are many lonely people living in immaculately clean houses.

Life is a collection of myriad minute details. The only way we can live our highest aspirations is by enfleshing them in our day-to-day attempts to love God and neighbor. There must be a growing unity between our highest spiritual ideals and our concrete moment-to-moment actions.

The little slices of everyday life have to be the vessels that carry spiritual ideals. An overly routinized existence shields us from essential questions about our human condition.

The more we come to appreciate the richness of the ordinary, the more eternal values enter into our temporal concerns. We place our routines in their proper relationship to our central goal: to seek first the kingdom of God to which all other goods shall be added (cf. Luke 12:31). In this process the Holy Spirit enkindles in us the fire of his love and casts out any fears and doubts that may still linger in our heart.

5

Feeling at Home

*Some people complain that they don't feel at home
in community because of a lack of understanding
and love. What can they do in such a situation?*

A house can have an aura of warmth and love about it, or it can
have a feeling of emptiness. Haven't we been to houses where we
were welcomed with food but still felt ill at ease? What are the reasons for such a feeling?

One cause that comes to mind might be an ambivalence I sense
in my hosts. They make the appropriate gestures of hospitality, but
they're not accompanied by real sincerity. They seem tense and
nervous, lacking in spontaneity.

The opposite is true of hosts or hostesses at home with themselves. Being at ease comes from a feeling of confidence and acceptance of self and others. Having integrated their gifts and their
flaws, they exhibit hospitality and humility. This lack of vanity
leaves room for loving trust in self, others, and God, resulting in a
gracious atmosphere of ease and welcome.

When we're at home with ourselves, we can more easily extend
the same feeling to others. In such a family or community, life is

congenial. By contrast, when we don't feel this gentle affirmation, we might unknowingly turn others off by our own inner ambivalence. They don't feel comfortable in our presence even though we might be doing everything we can "technically" do to make them feel at home.

Just as we must first love ourselves before we can love others, just as the unloved child is frightened of strangers, so the hesitant adult is anxious with outsiders. Ill at ease or gracious — it all depends on our sense of self-worth.

What are the ingredients that go into being at home? Security and a sense of belonging. Home, above all else, represents protection — a place where we can retreat from the trials of the outside world. For example, students can feel at home in the modest quarters they occupy during their college years. Books, papers, computers, a stray coffee cup or two — all attest to the fact that this simple room is their dwelling.

This contented feeling accompanies them when they leave the room to follow their daily schedule because they know they have a home to come to when the day is done. Attending classes, lunching with friends, jostling with the crowd intent upon catching the bus — none of these activities robs them of their feeling of homecoming. They know that part of this feeling has to do with a sense of security in their daily situation. Yet they can't say that the physical setting in which they find themselves constitutes this experience entirely. There's something deeper to consider.

One coed recalls being with her friends on a relaxing evening. The apartment was alive with spirited conversation. She contributed to the give-and-take — noticing the lively blend of silence and speech, of listening and responding, of being present to the others and to herself. "Being at home," she thought, "is simply being with one another." For all of us, it's the hum of friendly conversation, the smell of good cooking, the warm feeling of a company of friends together.

In the shelter of such memorable experiences, I enjoy a taste of the plentitude of life. Feeling at home isn't an emotion to define but an aura of familiarity, a sense of fitting together, of belonging, of harmony and order.

The home our parents provided for us as infants, the feelings of warmth and security we felt there, are sound models for our future homes. This original dwelling place became essential for our survival; we never outgrow our need for it.

While the security of home can provide relaxation and refreshment, it can also point to the unrealistic hope for a perfectly safe and complacent life. Home can make me feel so comfortable that I refuse to meet further challenges; it can cause a kind of fossilization whereby I take my life for granted and don't pay enough attention to what is new.

In this frame of mind, I can make home merely a secure nook of complacency out of which the true challenge of love has been drained. I close myself to the call to let go of self-centered needs so that I may grow in fresh ways of showing love. Such dying to self often entails the risk of being misunderstood and of having my ideas rejected from time to time.

Shoulder to shoulder with other human beings, I'm bound to encounter failure; I'm not going to accept everyone who comes my way or be accepted by them. I'm bound to encounter some rejection, no matter how loving a community is.

I might have unrealistic expectations of home life, seeking only fulfilling relationships without the inevitable suffering that accompanies self-giving love. When these expectations aren't met, I might feel compelled to leave home and seek the "idol of warm togetherness" elsewhere. Alas, that "elsewhere" never comes.

Am I Living a Spiritual Life?

Rejection and misunderstanding are part of the human condition. No change of residence will alter this fact.

As a Christian, I should be able to see that all genuine love comes through some dying to self. Often the feeling of being at home comes only after I pass through the crucible of alienation, disharmony, and non-acceptance. Although there's turmoil around me, I can still experience a sense of inner peace. If I don't feel quiet within, then no matter what anyone does to make me feel at home, it won't change my discomfort.

When I'm at home within myself, with my gifts and limits, I'm at rest. I find, with God's loving help, the courage to accept myself. While some aspects of life seem to be falling apart around me, I'm at peace because the Son of God himself lives in me and allows me to be who I am.

"Foxes have holes, and birds of the air have nests; but the Son of man has nowhere to lay his head" (Luke 9:58). That saying always strikes a plaintive chord in us. Christ seems to be declaring that he has no earthly home, that many will reject him, that foes won't allow him to make his home in their heart. What message does he offer to us in the haunting words: ". . . but the Son of man has nowhere to lay his head"?

Christ stayed at Peter's house. He was completely at home there. Days later, while the disciples were trembling in anticipation of the unknown and, afraid for their lives in a terrible storm, Jesus lay sound asleep in the boat. He was at home in the storm as well as on the shore (cf. Mark 4:35-41). Often he spent time in the house of his friends Martha, Mary, and Lazarus, where he felt totally at ease (cf. Luke 10:38-42). He seemed to be at home everywhere and yet nowhere in particular. When disciples ask if they can follow him, he warns them that he has nowhere to lay his head, as if that will be their lot as well.

How diligently, in this light, should I search for the perfect sense of being at home? At times Jesus was rejected by his own people. He lamented for Jerusalem, which had turned away from him (cf. Matt. 23:37-39). He suffered abandonment by his apostles when, in the Garden of Gethsemane, he most needed their company and begged them to watch with him for one hour (cf. Matt. 26:36).

As the Son of Man, he had no one place to call his own, not one to which he could return. Yet he had peace. He was at home with himself because of his union with his Father. He had come to do his will and then, as Son of God, he would return to his Father's house (cf. John 14:1-6).

In saying that he has nowhere to lay his head, Christ reminds us not to search for the perfect home here on earth. We must pass through the crucible of earthly limits into that joyous homecoming that lies beyond the present life. We must let go of our emotional need for any idealized place. We must be careful not to attach too much significance to harmonious togetherness, for all good things do come to an end.

The way of Christ is the only one that leads us to the Father's house. That is the shelter we Christians must ultimately seek.

6

Friendship in the Spiritual Life

What role does friendship play in the spiritual life?
Is it a help or a hindrance in our quest for union with God?

A true friend is a gift beyond price. Friendship can't be forced.
Like happiness, it might come to us as an unexpected blessing.

As we journey through life, many obstacles arise to block God's
grace. Selfism can keep people at a distance and separate us from
our Lord. We become preoccupied with our own universe. We
trust no one and move about as if we were our own savior. These
obstacles can be tempered when we're with a true friend, for
friendship calls us out of ourselves. As we allow others to share
our world and open our hearts to theirs, we transcend the narrow
confines selfishness always imposes.

To feel comfortable with a friend is to feel more at one with
myself. If our friendship is a healthy one, each of us becomes
strengthened to stand on our own feet. I know that my life is precious in my friend's eyes. His or her respect and love fill me with
gratitude and ready me for union with God.

When I'm with my friend, we sense the presence of God between us. Like the disciples on the road to Emmaus, our friendship

can be the occasion in which Jesus joins us in a special way (cf. Luke 24:13-32). In the face of discouragement, these two disciples remained together. They had given up everything and fled, but they hadn't abandoned each other. They held firm to their human relationship, even though their dreams and hopes were apparently shattered. Then they found the light. The Messiah whom they had considered to be so far off was as near to them as they were to one another.

Through this touching story, Jesus might be telling us to hold fast to those friendships that come to us as a pure gift. The challenges we encounter in the course of our friendship can teach us much about ourselves and the ways in which we do or don't understand one another.

When I first find a friend, I might be overjoyed at the many interests we share in common. It seems as if we're made of the same "stuff." Our friendship becomes a source of shared confirmation and call-appreciation.

As our friendship deepens, we sense ourselves being called forth in a new way. Disagreements might arise between us. In seeing each other's faults and weaknesses, we might feel disappointed, but, instead of thinking of these stumbling blocks as "the beginning of the end," we view them as just the beginning.

As we treat these points of disagreement agreeably, we find that our relationship grows stronger, not weaker. We admit that it's part of our human nature to be at times possessive of the other person, but we decide to let go of our expectations of perfectionism and work through our differences. Slowly we become purified of this clinging tendency. We grow in true respect and care for one another. Our love becomes more reasonable and realistic.

Growing in the art and discipline of spiritual friendship can teach us much about growing in relationship with God. When we first meet God in a personal way, we're as infatuated as a honeymooner with the promise of perfect bliss. So enamored are we of these signs of union that we fail to see the obstacles we must face on the way to lasting love. As we work through various barriers to grace, our love for God and for one another begins to enter into a stage of deeper communion.

Relationship with a friend can not only teach us to be more thoughtful, trusting, and caring; it can also help us become more open. This openness consists in our allowing the other to be who he or she is. Such letting be teaches us to grow in openness to God, whom we allow really to be God in our life. We stand in readiness to respond to the movements of grace wherever they lead.

Regarding this point, a poster reads, "A friend sees you through even when he or she sees through you." A friend is someone with whom I can talk about things that really concern me. I don't have to be afraid of saying something stupid or foolish, nor do I have to try to be eloquent or impressive. If I did, my friend would see through such ploys anyway.

With my friend, I don't have to be someone I'm not in order to be liked. I can be the imperfect self I am and still feel confirmed. This confirmation doesn't lead me to become stubbornly embedded in who I am now or in what I do. Friendship helps me to grow from one phase of maturity to the next.

My friend sees me through — through a bad mood, through a trying experience, through a matter about which we have disagreed. I might feel his or her support in kind words, through a helping hand, a concerned confrontation, or a stimulating argument. My friend sees me through to what I can become — no matter how slowly I stumble along.

An obstacle to grace I place upon myself is the feeling that I must make myself worthy of God's love, that I must earn God's favor. I feel as if I have to be perfect. If I make a mistake, if I fail, I think it means that I might fall into divine disfavor. I become tense and anxious. I'm alone in my striving. I have to perfect myself so that I can be worthy to receive God's grace.

Such willfulness has no place in our relationship with God. Grace is a gift given to me before I do anything. God is present to me in my imperfection. His love embraces me even when I'm unfaithful or forgetful.

God's grace works through who I am now. It doesn't wait until I become who I'd like to be. My role is to maintain an attitude of receptivity and to accept humbly God's loving presence in my life.

The graciousness of God, his generosity, can be overwhelming. It can be almost too much for me to conceive. The whole atmosphere in which I live says I have to compete for what I get. I have to earn it. No wonder I find it difficult to experience this pure gift.

Although it's a faint image, my relationship with my friend reflects in some measure my relationship with God. God sees through me perfectly. He sees me as I can never see myself — in all my superficiality and frailty — yet his vision goes beyond those flaws to my deepest center. Although I'm prone to mar the image he has made, God sees me through.

Friendship can be a facilitating condition for spiritual growth. A friend can open my eyes to the beauty of others and to my own special gifts as well as enabling me to become more aware of my blind spots. In the pain that's part of any true relationship, I can learn generosity, other-centeredness, and compassion. My hope is that I may be able to give and receive love in the real world, aware of our mutual limits and unafraid of our imperfections.

A close friendship can educate me to greater detachment from my own agenda. I'm there to allow the other to fulfill the mystery of his or her unique calling, even if that means missing some times of our togetherness. If I'm without a close friend, this situation shouldn't send me on a panicky search for the "perfect other." My challenge might be to grow closer to God through solitude and through being more open to the call to inclusive love. If I'm blessed with a friendship "made in heaven," I need to remain conscious of its finite character, never forgetting the infinite horizon of which our affection is but a dim mirror.

Spiritual friendship can melt away many obstacles to a deeper relationship with God and others on the condition that our love for one another increases our love and longing for God. Only then can our friendship be an avenue to spiritual deepening. My friend and I need to be aware of the limited nature of any human encounter. We have to hold our hearts in readiness for the love that lasts through this life and into the next, claiming and giving absolutely everything.

True friendship is a wonderful aid to bringing out the "flaws" in each other's personality that keep us from being our best selves. For example, I might need to have the final say in every situation, but my friend shows me, despite my gifts, where I'm limited. I might find it difficult to communicate with certain individuals, but my friend teaches me how to appreciate the talents they have.

Friendship is made more pristine by our common goal to live in union with Christ, who reveals to us the way to interact in genuine love for one another and for those with whom we live and work. In the words of Antoine Saint-Exupéry, "Love does not consist in gazing at each other . . . but in looking outward together in the same direction."

About the Authors

SUSAN MUTO

Susan Muto, Ph.D., executive director of the Epiphany Association and a native of Pittsburgh, is a renowned speaker, author, teacher, and dean of the Epiphany Academy of Formative Spirituality. A single laywoman living her vocation in the world and doing full-time, church-related ministry in the Epiphany Association, she has led conferences, seminars, workshops, and institutes throughout the world.

Professor Muto received her Ph.D. in English literature from the University of Pittsburgh, where she specialized in the work of post-Reformation spiritual writers. Beginning in 1966, she served in various administrative positions at the Institute of Formative Spirituality (IFS) at Duquesne University and taught as a full professor in its programs, edited its journals, and served as its director from 1981 to 1988. An expert in literature and spirituality, she continues to teach courses on an adjunct basis at many schools, seminaries, and centers of higher learning. She aims in her teaching to integrate the life of prayer and presence with professional ministry and in-depth formation in the home, the church, and the marketplace.

As coeditor of *Epiphany Connexions*, *Epiphany Inspirations*, and *Epiphany International*, as a frequent contributor to scholarly and popular journals, and as the author and coauthor of more than thirty books, Dr. Muto keeps up to date with the latest developments in her field. In fact, her many books on formative reading of scripture and the masters are considered to be premier introductions to the basic, classical art and discipline of spiritual formation and its systematic, comprehensive, formation theology. She lectures nationally and internationally on the treasured wisdom of the Judeo-Christian faith and formation tradition and on many foundational facets of living human and Christian values in today's world. Professor Muto holds membership in numerous honorary organizations and has received many distinctions for her work, including a Doctor of Humanities degree from King's College in Wilkes-Barre, Pennsylvania.

ADRIAN VAN KAAM

Fr. Adrian van Kaam, C.S.Sp., Ph.D., is the originator of formation science and its underlying formation anthropology. These new disciplines serve his systematic and systemic formation theology. Taken as a whole, all three fields comprise the art and discipline he named formative spirituality.

He inaugurated this unique approach in Holland in the 1940s. Upon coming to the United States in 1954, he went to Case Western Reserve University in Cleveland, where he received his doctorate in psychology. Shortly thereafter he became an American citizen. From 1954 to 1963, he taught his original approach to psychology as a human science at Duquesne University. Then in 1963 he founded the graduate Institute of Formative Spirituality, received the President's Award for excellence in research, and taught there as a professor in this field until its closing in 1993. He's also the recipient of an honorary Doctor of Christian Letters degree from the Franciscan University of Steubenville, Ohio.

About the Authors

Fr. Adrian, a renowned speaker and an inspiration to many, is the author of numerous books on spiritual formation and a prolific poet whose works enjoy worldwide recognition. Currently he serves as senior researcher and chaplain-in-residence of the Epiphany Academy of Formative Spirituality, which he co-founded with Dr. Susan Muto as part of their over twenty-five-year commitment to the Epiphany Association and its worldwide mission and ministry.

Sophia Institute Press®

Sophia Institute is a nonprofit institution that seeks to restore man's knowledge of eternal truth, including man's knowledge of his own nature, his relation to other persons, and his relation to God. Sophia Institute Press® serves this end in numerous ways: it publishes translations of foreign works to make them accessible for the first time to English-speaking readers; it brings out-of-print books back into print; and it publishes important new books that fulfill the ideals of Sophia Institute. These books afford readers a rich source of the enduring wisdom of mankind.

Sophia Institute Press® makes these high-quality books available to the general public by using advanced technology and by soliciting donations to subsidize its general publishing costs. Your generosity can help Sophia Institute Press® to provide the public with editions of works containing the enduring wisdom of the ages. Please send your tax-deductible contribution to the address below. We welcome your questions, comments, and suggestions.

For your free catalog, call:
Toll-free: 1-800-888-9344

Sophia Institute Press®
Box 5284 • Manchester, NH 03108
www.sophiainstitute.com

Sophia Institute® is a tax-exempt institution as defined by the Internal Revenue Code, Section 501(c)(3). Tax I.D. 22-2548708.